D1636789

Held for Orders

Shockley

Held for Orders

Being

Stories of Railroad Life

By

Frank H. Spearman

Illustrations by
JAY HAMBIDGE

Held for Orders was Frank Spearman's second collection of western "railroad" short stories (following *The Nerve of Foley*). It was reprinted a number of times, including by the reprint publisher, A. L. Burt. However, original copies are hard to find, indicating that the press runs were probably not large. "The Yellow Mail," one of the best stories in the book, was turned into a film in 1927. (A number of Spearman's stories and novels were turned into films, the best known of which is "Whispering Smith" starring Alan Ladd.) *Held for Orders* introduces the "Medicine Bend" locale which is continued in his novels, *The Daughter of a Magnate* (1903) and *Whispering Smith* (1906).   —F.W.

Originally published by McClure, Phillips & Company, 1901

Published by
The Paper Tiger, Inc.
335 Jefferson Avenue
Cresskill, NJ 07626
(201) 567-5620

ISBN 1-889439-00-2

To

John Francis Cordeal

Contents

Illustrations

Held for Orders

The Switchman's Story

SHOCKLEY

The Switchman's Story

SHOCKLEY

H E's rather a bad lot, I guess," wrote Bucks
to Callahan, "but I am satisfied of one
thing — you can't run that yard with a
Sunday-school superintendent. He won't make you
any trouble unless he gets to drinking. If that
happens, *don't have any words with him*." Bucks
underscored three times. "Simply crawl into a
cyclone cellar and wire me. Sending you eighteen
loads of steel to-night, and six cars of ties. Blair
reports section 10 ready for track layers and Mear's
outfit moving into the Palisade Cañon. Push the
stuff to the front."

It was getting dark, and Callahan sat in that part
of the Benkleton depot he called the office, pulling

at a muddy root that went unaccountably hot in
sudden flashes.   He took the pipe from his mouth,
leaving his foot on the table, and looked at the bowl
resentfully, wondering again if there could be powder in that infernal tobacco of Rubedo's.   The mouthpiece he eyed as a desperate man might ponder a
final shift.

The pipe had originally come from God's Country, with a Beautiful Amber Mouthpiece, and a Beautiful Bowl; but it was a present from his sister and
had been bought at a dry-goods store.   Once when
thinking — or, if you please, when not thinking —
Callahan had held a lighted match to the Beautiful
Amber Mouthpiece instead of to the tobacco, and
in the fire that ensued they had hard work to save
the depot.

Callahan never wrote his sister about it; he
thought only about buying pipes at dry-goods stores,
and about being, when they exploded, a thousand
miles from the man who sold them.   There was
plenty in that to think about.   What he now brought
his teeth reluctantly together on was part of the rub-

ber tube of a dismantled atomizer; in happier post-Christmas days a toilet fixture. But Callahan had abandoned the use of bay rum after shaving. His razor had gone to the scrap and on Sunday mornings he merely ran a pair of scissors over the high joints — for Callahan was railroading — and on the front.

After losing the mouthpiece he would have been completely in the air but for little Chris Oxen. Chris was Callahan's section gang. His name was once Ochsner, but that wasn't in Benkleton. Callahan was hurried when he made up the pay roll and put it Oxen, as being better United States. I say United States because Callahan said United States, in preference to English.

Chris had been in America only three years; but he had been in Russia three hundred, and in that time had learned many ways of getting something out of nothing. When the red-haired despatcher after the explosion cast away with bitterness the remains of the pipe, Chris picked it up and by judicious action on the atomizer figured out a new

mouthpiece no worse than the original, for while
the second, like the first, was of rubber, it was not
of the explosive variety.

Chris presented the remodelled root to Callahan as
a surprise; Callahan, in a burst of gratitude, promoted him on the spot : he made little Chris foreman.   It did n't bring any advance in pay — but
there was the honor.   To be foreman was an
honor, and as little Chris was the only man on the
yard force, he became, by promotion, foreman of
himself.

So Callahan sat thinking of the ingenuity of Chris,
reflecting on the sting of construction tobacco, and
studying over Bucks's letter.

The yard was his worry.   Not that it was much
of a yard; just a dozen runs off the lead to take
the construction material for Callahan to distribute,
fast as the grade was pushed westward.   The trouble at the Benkleton yard came from without, not
from within.

The road was being pushed into the cattle country,
and it was all easy till they struck Benkleton.   Ben-

kleton was just a hard knot on the Yellow Grass
trail: a squally, sandy cattle town.   There were
some bad men in Benkleton; they did n't bother
often.   But there were some men in Benkleton
who thought they were bad, and these were
a source of constant bedevilment to the railroad
men.

Southwest of the yard, where the river breaks
sheer into the bottoms, there hived and still hives a
colony of railroad laborers, Russians.   They have
squatted there, burrowed into the face of the bench
like sand swallows, and scraped caves out for themselves, and the name of the place is Little Russia.

This was in the troublous days, when the cowboys,
homesick for evil, would ride around Little Russia
with rope and gun, and scare the pioneers cross-eyed.
The cattle fellows spent the entire winter months,
all sand and sunshine, putting up schemes to worry
Callahan and the Little Russians.   The headquarters for this restless gang were at Pat Barlie's place,
across from the post office ; it was there that the
cowboys loved to congregate.   To Callahan, Pat

Barlie's place was a wasps' nest; but to Chris, it was a den of wolves — and of a dreader sort than Russian wolves, for Barlie's pack never slept.

The east and west section men could run away from them on hand cars; it was the yardmen who caught it, and it grew so bad they could n't keep a switchman. About ten o'clock at night, after Number Twenty-three had pulled in and they were distributing a trainload of bridge timber, a switch-man's lantern would go up in signal, when *pist!* a bullet would knock the lamp clean out of his hand, and the nerve clean out of his head. Handling a light in the Benkleton yard was like smoking a cel-luloid pipe — you never could tell when it would go off.

Cowboys shot away the lamps faster than requisi-tions could be drawn for new ones. They shot the signals off the switches, and the lights from the tops of moving trains. Whenever a brakeman showed a flicker, two cowboys stood waiting to snuff it. If they missed the lamp, they winged the brakeman. It compelled Bucks after a while to run trains through

Benkleton without showing ever a light. This, though tough, could be managed, but to shunt flats in the yard at night with no light, or to get a switchman willing to play young Tell to Peg Leg Reynolds's William for any length of time, was impossible. At last Bucks, on whom the worry reflected at headquarters, swore he would fight them with fire, and he sent Shockley. Callahan still sat speculating on what he would be up against when Shockley arrived.

The impression Bucks's letter gave him — knowing Bucks to be frugal of words — was that Shockley would rise up with cartridges in his ears and bowie knives dangling from his watch chain. To live in fear of the cowboys was one thing; but to live in fear of the cowboys on the one hand, and in terror of a yard master on the other, seemed, all things considered, confusing, particularly if the new ally got to drinking and his fire scattered. Just then train Fifty-nine whistled. Pat Barlie's corner began to sputter its salute. Callahan shifted around behind his bombproof, lit his powder horn, and looking down the line wondered whether Shockley might be on that train.

It was not till the next night though that a tall, thinnish chap, without visible reasons for alighting, got off Fifty-nine and walked tentatively down the platform. At the ticket office he asked for the assistant superintendent.

" Out there on the platform talking to the conductor."

The thin fellow emerged and headed for Callahan. Callahan noticed only his light, springy amble and his hatchet face.

" Mr. Callahan ? "

" Yes."

" Bucks sent me up — to take the yard."

" What 's your name ? "

" Shockley."

" Step upstairs. I 'll be up in a minute."

Shockley walked back into the depot but he left the copper-haired assistant superintendent uncertain as to whether it was really over ; whether Shockley had actually arrived or not. As Callahan studied the claimant's inoffensive appearance, walking away, he rather thought it could n't be over, or that Bucks was mistaken ; but Bucks never made a mistake.

Next morning at seven, the new yard master took hold. Callahan had intimated that the night air in the yard, it being low land, was miasmatic, and that Shockley had maybe better try for a while to do his switching in the daytime. Just before the appointed hour in the morning, the assistant had looked out on his unlucky yard ; he thought to himself that if that yard did n't drive a man to drink nothing ever would. Piled shanty high with a bewildering array of material, it was enough to take the heart out of a Denver switching crew.

While he stood at the window he saw their plug switch engine, that had been kicked out of every other yard on the system, wheeze out of the round-house, saw the new yard master flirt his hand at the engineer, and swing up on the footboard. But the swing — it made Callahan's heart warm to him. Not the lubberly jump of the hoboes that had worried the life out of him all summer, even when the cattlemen did n't bother. It was the swing of the sailor into the shrouds, of the Cossack into the saddle, of the yacht into the wind. It was like falling down or falling up or falling on — the grace of a mastery of gravitation — that was Shockley's swing on the foot-board of the yard engine as it shot snorting past him.

" He 's all right," muttered Callahan. It was enough.

A man who flipped a tender like that was not like to go very wrong even in that chaos of rails and ties and stringers and coal.

" Now," continued Callahan to himself, timidly hopeful, " if the cuss only does n't get to drinking ! " He watched apprehensively, dreading the first time he should see him entering Pat Barlie's place, but Shockley did n't appear to know Pat had a place. The cowboys, too, watched him, waiting for his lamp to gleam at night down in the yard, but their patience was strained for a long time. Shockley got all his work done by daylight.

To the surprise of Callahan, and probably on the principle of the watched pot, the whole winter went

without a brush between Shockley and the cowboys.
Even Peg Leg Reynolds let him alone. "He's the
luckiest fellow on earth," remarked Callahan one day
at McCloud in reply to a question from Bucks about
Shockley. "There has n't a shot been fired at him
all winter."

"He was n't always lucky," commented Bucks,
signing a batch of letters.

"He came from Chicago," Bucks went on, after
a silence. "He was switching there on the 'Q' at
the time of the stock-yards riots. Shockley used to
drink like a pirate. I never knew just the right of
it. I understood it was in a brawl — anyway, he
killed a man there; shot him, and had to get away
in a hurry. I was train master. Shockley was a
striker; but I'd always found him decent, and
when his wife came to me about it I helped
her out a little; she's dead since. His record
is n't just right back there yet. There's something about the shooting hanging over him. I
never set eyes on the fellow again till he struck
me for a job at McCloud; then I sent him up to

you. He claimed he 'd quit drinking — guess he had. Long as he 's behaving himself I believe in giving him a chance — h'm ? ''

It really was n't any longer a case of giving him a chance ; rather of whether they could get on without him. When the Colorado Pacific began racing us into Denver that summer, it began to crowd even Shockley to keep the yard clean ; he saw he would have to have help.

" Chris, what do they give you for tinkering up the ties ? " asked Shockley one day.

" Dollar an' a half."

" Why don't you take hold switching with me and get three dollars ? "

Chris was thunderstruck. First he said Callahan would n't let him, but Shockley " guessed yes." Then Chris figured. To save the last of the hundred dollars necessary to get the woman and the babies over — it could be done in three months instead of six, if only Callahan would listen. But when Shockley talked Callahan always listened, and when he asked for a new switchman he got him. And

Chris got his three; to him a sum unspeakable. By the time the woman and the children arrived in the fall, Chris would have died for Shockley.

The fall that saw the woman and the stunted subjects of the Czar stowed away under the bench in Little Russia brought also the cowboys down from Montana to bait the Russians.

One stormy night, when Chris thought it was perfectly safe to venture up to Rubedo's after groceries, the cowboys caught him and dragged him over to Pat Barlie's.

It was seven when they caught him, and by nine they had put him through every pace that civilization could suggest. Peg Leg Reynolds, as always, master of ceremonies, then ordered him tied to the stove. When it was done, the cowboys got into a big circle for a dance. The fur on Chris's coat had already begun to sizzle, when the front door opened. Shockley walked in.

Straight, in his ambling, hurried way, he walked past the deserted bar through the ring of cowboys at the rear to Chris frying against the stove, and began cutting him loose. Through every knot that his knife slit he sent a very loud and very bad word, and no sooner had he freed Chris than he jerked him by the collar, as if quarreling with him, toward the back door, which was handy, and before the cow-boys got wind he had shoved him through it.

"Hold on there!" cried Peg Leg Reynolds, when it was just too late. Chris was out of it, and Shockley turned alone.

"All right, partner; what is it?" he asked amiably.

"You've got a ripping nerve."

"I know it."

"What's your name?"

"Shockley."

"Can you dance?"

"No."

It was Peg Leg's opportunity. He drew his gun. "I reckon maybe you can. Try it," he added, point-ing the suggestion with the pistol. Shockley looked foolish; he did n't begin tripping soon enough, and a bullet from the cowboy's gun splintered the base-board at his feet. Shockley attempted to shuffle.

To any one who did n't know him it looked funny. But Peg Leg was a rough dancing master, and before he said enough an ordinary man would have dropped exhausted.   Shockley, breathing a good bit quicker, only steadied himself against the bar.

"Take off your hat before gentlemen," cried the cowboy.   Shockley hesitated, but he did pull off his cap.

"That 's more like it.   What 's your name?"

"Shockley."

"Shockley?" echoed Reynolds with a burst of range amenities.   "Well, Shockley, you can't help your name.   Drink for once in your life with a man of breeding — my name 's Reynolds.   Pat, set out the good bottle — this guy pays," exclaimed Peg Leg, wheeling to the bar.

"What 'll it be?" asked Pat Barlie of Shockley, as he deftly slid a row of glasses in front of the men of breeding.

"Ginger ale for me," suggested Shockley mildly. The cowboys put up a single yell.   Ginger ale! It was too funny.

Reynolds, choking with contempt, pointed to the yard master's glass. " Fill it with whiskey," he shouted. "Fill it, Pat!" he repeated, as Shockley leaned undecidedly against the bar.   The yard master held out the glass, and the bar keeper began to pour.   Shockley looked at the liquor a moment; then he looked at Reynolds, who fronted him gun in one hand and red water in the other.

" Drink ! "

Shockley paused, looked again at the whiskey and drew the glass towards him with the curving hand of a drinker.   " You want me to drink this ? " he half laughed, turning on his baiter.

" I did n't say so, did I ? I said DRINK ! " roared Peg Leg.

Everybody looked at Shockley.   He stood fingering the glass quietly.   Somehow everybody, drunk or sober, looked at Shockley.   He glanced around at the crowd; other guns were creeping from their holsters.   He pushed the glass back, smiling.

" I don't drink whiskey, partner," said Shockley gently.

" You 'll drink that whiskey, or I 'll put a little hole into you ! ' "

Shockley reached good-naturedly for the glass, threw the liquor on the floor, and set it back on the bar.

" Go on ! " said Shockley. It confused Reynolds.

" A man that 'll waste good whiskey ought n't t' live, anyhow," he muttered, fingering his revolver nervously. " You 've spoiled my aim. Throw up your hat," he yelled. " I 'll put a hole through that to begin with."

Instead, Shockley put his cap back on his head.

" Put a hole through it there," said he. Reynolds set down his glass, and Shockley waited; it was the cowboy who hesitated.

" Where 's your nerve ? " asked the railroad man. The gun covered him with a flash and a roar. Reynolds, whatever his faults, was a shot. His bullet cut cleanly through the crown, and the powder almost burnt Shockley's face. The switchman recovered himself instantly, and taking off his cap laughed as he examined the hole.

" Done with me ? " he asked evenly, cap in hand.

Peg Leg drained his glass before he spoke. " Get out ! " he snapped. The switchman started on the word for the front door. When he opened it, everybody laughed — but Shockley.

Maybe an hour later Reynolds was sitting back of the stove in a card game, when a voice spoke at his ear. "Get up!" Reynolds looked around into a pistol; behind it stood Shockley, pleasant. "Get up ! " he repeated. Nobody had seen him come in; but there he was, and with an absolutely infantile gun, a mere baby gun, in the yellow light, but it shone like bright silver.

Reynolds with visible embarrassment stood up.

" Throw your cannon into the stove, Reynolds, you won't need it," suggested Shockley. Reynolds looked around; there appeared to be no hopeful alternative: the drop looked very cold; not a cowboy interposed. Under convoy, Reynolds stumped over to the stove and threw in his gun, but the grace of the doing was bad.

" Get up there on the bar and dance ; hustle ! " urged Shockley. They had to help the confused

Chris:

cowboy up; and when he stood shamefaced, looking down on the scene of his constant triumphs,
and did a painful single foot, marking time with
his peg, the cowboys, who had stood their own
share of his bullying, roared. Shockley did n't
roar; only stood with busy eyes where he could
cover any man on demand, not forgetting even Pat
Barlie.

Peg Leg, who had danced so many in his day,
danced, and his roasting gun sputtered an accom-
paniment from the stove; but as Shockley, who
stood in front of it, paid no attention to the
fusillade of bullets, good form prevented others
from dodging. "That 'll do; get down. Come
here, Chris," called Shockley. Chris Oxen, greatly
disturbed, issued from an obscure corner.

"Get down on your knees," exclaimed the yard
master, jerking Reynolds with a chilly twist in
front of the frightened Russian. "Get on your
knees; right where I threw your whiskey," and
Shockley, crowding Reynolds down to his humilia-
tion, dropped for the first time into range civilities

himself, and the shame and the abasement of it were very great.

" Boys," said the yard master, with one restless eye on Reynolds and one on everybody else, as he pointed at Chris, " this man's coat was burnt up. He's a poor devil, and his money comes hard. Chip in for a new coat. I 've nothing against any man that don't want to give, but Reynolds must pass the hat. Take mine, you coyote."

Nearly everybody contributed as Reynolds went round. Shockley made no comments. " Count it," he commanded, when the fallen monarch had finished ; and when the tale was made, Shockley told Pat Barlie to put in as much more as the cap held, and he did so.

" There, Chris ; go home. I don't like you," added Shockley, insolently, turning on Reynolds. " You don't know what fun is. This town won't hold you and me after to-night. You can take it or you can leave it, but the first time I ever put eyes on you again one of us will cash in."

He backed directly towards the front door and out.

Peg Leg Reynolds took only the night to decide;
next day he hit the trail. The nervy yard master
he might have wiped out if he had stayed, but the
disgrace of kneeling before the dog of a Russian
was something never to be wiped out in the annals
of Benkleton. Peg Leg moved on; and thereafter
cowboys took occasion to stop Shockley on the
street and jolly him on the way he did the one-
legged bully, and the lights were shot no more.

The railroad men swore by the new yard master;
the Russians took their cigarettes from their mouths
and touched their caps when Shockley passed;
Callahan blessed his name; but little Chris wor-
shiped him.

One day Alfabet Smith dropped off at Benkleton
from Omaha headquarters. Alfabet was the only
species of lizard on the pay roll — he was the
West End spotter. "Who is that slim fellow?"
he asked of Callahan as Shockley flew by on the
pilot board of an engine.

"That 's Shockley."

"Oh, that 's Shockley, is it?"

But he could say little things in a way to make a man prick hot all over.

" Yes, that 's Shockley. Why ? " asked Callahan with a dash of acid.

" Nothing, only he 's a valuable man; he 's wanted, Shockley is," smiled Alfabet Smith, but his smile would freeze tears.

Callahan took it up short. " Look here, Alfabet. Keep off Shockley."

" Why ? "

" Why ? Because you and I will touch, head on, if you don't."

Smith said nothing; he was used to that sort. The next time Bucks was up, his assistant told him of the incident.

" If he bothers Shockley," Bucks said, " we 'll get his scalp, that 's all. He 'd better look after his conductors and leave our men alone."

" I notice Shockley is n't keeping his frogs blocked," continued Bucks, reverting to other matters. " That won't do. I want every frog in the yard blocked and kept blocked, and tell him I said so."

But the frog-blocking was not what worried Shockley; his push was to keep the yard clean, for the month of December brought more stuff twice over than was ever poured into the front-end yard before. Chris, though, had developed into a great switchman, and the two never let the work get ahead.

So it came that Little Russia honored Chris and his big pay check above most men. Shockley stood first in Little Russia; then the CZAR, then Chris, then Callahan. Queen Victoria and Bismarck might have admirers; but they were not in it under the bench.

When the Russian holidays came, down below, Chris concluded that the celebration would be merely hollow without Shockley; for was not the very existence of Little Russia due to him? All the growth, all the prosperity — what was it due to? Protection. What was the protection? Shockley. There were brakemen who argued that protection came from the tariff; but they never made any converts in Little Russia, where the inhabitants could be induced to

vote for president only on the assurance that Shockley
was running.

"Well, what's the racket anyhow, Chris?" demanded Shockley lazily, after Cross-Eyes trying to
get rid of the invitation to the festivities had sputtered switch-English five minutes at him.

"Ve got Chrismus by us," explained Chris des-
perately.

"Christmas," repeated Shockley grimly. "Christmas.   Why, man, Christmas don't come nowhere
on earth in January.   You want to wind up your
calendar.   Where 'd you get them shoes?"

"Dollar sefenty-vife."

"Where?"

"Rubedo."

"And don't you know a switchman ought n't t'
put his feet in flatboats?   Don't you know some day
you 'll get your foot stuck in a tongue or a guard?
Then where 'll you be, Dutch, with a string of flats
rolling down on you, eh?"

However, Chris stuck for his request.   He
would n't take no for an answer.   Next day he
tired Shockley out.

"Well, for God's sake let up, Chris," said the yard master at last. "I 'll come down a while after Twenty-three comes in. Get back early after supper, and we 'll make up Fifty-five and let the rest go."

It was a pretty night; pretty enough over the yard for anybody's Christmas, Julian or Gregorian. No snow, but a moon, and a full one, rising early over the Arikaree bluffs, and a frost that bit and sparkled, and the north wind asleep in the sand hills.

Shockley, after supper, snug in a pea-jacket and a storm cap, rode with the switch engine down from the roundhouse. Chris, in his astrakhan reefer and turban, walking over from the dugouts in Rubedo's new shoes, flipped the footboard at the stock-yard with almost the roll of Shockley himself.

Happily for Christmas in Little Russia, Twenty-three pulled in on time; but it was long and heavy that night. It brought coal and ties, and the stuff for the Fort Rawlins depot, and a batch of bridge steel they had been waiting two weeks for— mostly Cherry Creek stuff— eleven cars of it.

The minute the tired engine was cut off the long train, up ran the little switch engine and snapped at the headless monster like a coyote.

Out came the coal with a clatter; out came the depot stuff with a sheet of flame through the goat's flues — shot here, shot there, shot yonder — flying down this spur and down that and the other, like stones from a catapult; and the tough-connected, smut-faced, blear-eyed yard engine coughed and snorted and spit a shower of sparks and soot and cinders up into the Christmas air. She darted and dodged and jerked, and backed up and down and across the lead, and never for a fraction of a second took her eye off Shockley's lamp. Shivering and clanging and bucking with steam and bell and air, but always with one smoky eye on Shockley's lamp, until Twenty-three was wrecked clean to the caboose, and the switch engine shot down the main line with the battered way-car in her claws like a hawk with a prairie dog.

Then there was only the west-bound freight, Fifty-five, to make up with the Fort Rawlins stuff and the Cherry Creek steel, which was " *rush*,"and a few cars of ties flung on behind on general principles. It was quick work now — sorting and moving the bridge steel — half an hour for an hour's work, with the north wind waking at the clatter and sweeping a bank of cloud and sand across the valley. Shockley and Chris and the goat crew put at it like black ants. There was releasing and setting and kicking and splitting, and once in a while a flying switch, dead against the rubrics; and at last the whole train of steel was in line, clean as the links of a sprocket, and ready to run in on the house-track for the caboose.

For that run Chris set the east house-track switch, crossed the track, and swung a great circle with his lamp for the back. To get over to the switch again, he started to recross the track. In the dark his ankle turned on a lump of coal; he recovered lightly, but the misstep sent his other foot wide, and with a bit of a jolt Rubedo's new shoe slipped into the frog.

Up the track he heard a roll of stormy coughs from

the engine gathering push to shove the string of
flats down. They were coming towards him, over
the spot where he stood, on his signal; and he
quietly tried to loosen his heel.

The engine's drivers let go, and she roared a
steaming oath, and Chris could hear it; but he
was glad, for his heel would not work quietly out
of the frog; it stuck. Then the engineer, un-
ruffled, pulled at his sand lever, and his engine
snorted again and her driver tires bit, and slowly
she sent the long train of steel down on Chris's
switch; he heard the frosty flanges grinding on
the face of the rails as he tried to loosen his
foot.

Coolly, first, like a confident man in a quicksand;
soon, with alarm running into fright. But there
was time enough; the head car was four or five
lengths above the switch and coming very, very
slowly, heavy-like, and squeaking stiffly under its
load, yet coming; and he wrenched harder, but his
foot stuck. Then he yelled for Shockley. Shockley had gone over to open the caboose switch;

Shockley could n't hear, and he knew it. And he yelled again.

The sweat broke over him as he turned and twisted. The grip of the frog seemed to stifle him ; half the time was gone ; the near truck wheels screeched two car-lengths away : and the switchman played his last card. Time and time again Shockley had told him what to do if that moment came in the night ; had told him to throw his lamp in the air like a rocket. But Chris had forgotten all that till the flat dropped heavily on the tongue in front of him ; then he threw his lamp like a rocket high into the night.

No help came. He raised his arms frantically above his head, and his cries cut the wind. Desperate at last, he threw himself flat to lie outside the rail, to save all but a foot ; but the frog held him, and crying horribly he struggled back to his feet, only to sink again half crazy to the ground. As his senses left him he was hardly aware of a stinging pain in his foot, of a wrench at his leg, an instant arm round his back, and his yard master's voice in his ear.

" Jump ! " screamed Shockley.

Chris, scrambling frantically on the deadly rails, unable to jump, felt himself picked from the ground, heard a choke in the throat at his ear, and he was flung like a drawbar through the dark. Shockley had passed a knife blade from vamp to sole, slit the Russian's clumsy shoe, jerked his foot from it, and thrown him bodily into the clear.

Chris staggered panting to his feet. Already the steel was moving slowly over the switch; he heard the sullen pounding of the trucks on the contact; a lantern, burning yet, lay on its side near the stand — it was Shockley's lamp. Chris looked wildly around for his yard master; called out; called Shockley's name; listened. No scream, no groan, no cry, no answer; no sound, but just the steady pounding of the wheels over the contact. The little switchman screamed again in a frenzy, and turning, raced stumbling up the track to the cab. He swung into it, and by signs made the engineer shut off. He tried to talk, and only stammered a lingo of switch-pidgin and the name

of Shockley. They could n't understand it all, but
they shut off with faces pinched and sallow, threw
open the furnace door, and grabbing their lanterns
ran back. The fireman on his knees held his
lamp out under the flat that spanned the contact ;
he drew shrinking back, and rising, started on the
run for the depot to rouse Callahan.

It was Callahan who pulled the pin a moment later,
Chris shivering like a rabbit at his side. It was
Callahan who gave the slow pull-ahead order that
cut the train in two at the frog, and Callahan who
stepped wavering from the gap that opened behind
the receding flat — back from something between
the rails — back to put his hands blindly out
for the target-rod, and unsteadily upon it. He
heard Shockley breathing.

Some carried the headlight back, and some tore the
door off a box car, and they got him on. They
carried him unevenly, stumbling, over to the depot.
They laid him on Callahan's mattress in the waiting room, and the men stood all about him ; but
the only sound was his breathing, and inside under

the lamp the receiver, clicking, clicking, clicking, of Bucks and the company surgeon coming on a special ahead of Fifty-nine.

They twisted tourniquets into his quivering flesh, and with the light dying in his eyes they put whiskey to his lips. But he turned his head and spit it from his mouth. Then he looked from face to face about him — to the engineer and to the fireman, and to little Chris and to Callahan, and his lips moved.

Chris bent over him, but try as he would he could not catch the words. And Callahan listened and watched and waited.

" Block — block — " said Shockley's lips. And Callahan wiped them slowly and bent close again and put his ear over them. " Block — block — the — frogs."

And Shockley died.

They lifted the mattress into the baggage room; Callahan drew over it a crumpled sheet. A lantern left, burned on the checking desk, but the men, except Chris, went their ways. Chris hung irresolute around the open door.

The special pulled in, and with the shoes wringing fire from her heels as she slowed, Bucks and a man following close sprang from the step of the coach. Callahan met them; shook his head.

Twenty minutes later Fifty-nine whistled for the yard; but in the yard all was dark and still. One man got off Fifty-nine that night. Carrying his little valise in his hand, he walked in and out of the depot, hanging on the edges of the grouping men, who still talked of the accident. After hearing, he walked alone into the baggage room, and with his valise in his hand drew back the edge of the sheet and, standing, looked. Afterward he paused at the door, and spoke to a man that was fixing a lantern.

"What was his name?"

"Shockley."

"Shockley?"

"Yes."

"Yard master here?"

"Yes. Know him?"

"Me? No. I guess not." He walked away with his valise, and drew his coat collar up in the wind that swept the platform. "I guess I don't want him," he muttered to himself. " I guess *they* don't want *him ;* not now." And he went back to the man and asked when a train left again for Chicago. He had a warrant for Shockley; but Shockley's warrant had been served.

After the others had gone, Bucks and Callahan and the surgeon talked together in the waiting room, and Chris hanging by, blear-eyed and helpless, looked from one to the other : showed his foot when Callahan pointed, and sat patient while the surgeon stitched the slit where Shockley's blade had touched the bone. Then he stood again and listened. While any one talked Chris would listen ; silent and helpless, just listening. And when Bucks had gone up stairs, and the surgeon had gone up stairs, and Callahan, tired and sick, had gone up stairs, and only the operator sat under his lamp at the table, Chris stood back in the gloom in front of the stove and poked stealthily at the fire. When it blazed he dropped big chunks of smutty coal in on it, and wiped his frost-bitten nose with the back of his

dirty hand, and looked toward the baggage room
door and listened — listened for a cry, or a sound,
or for that fearful, fearful breathing, such breathing
as he had not been hearing before. But no cry, no
sound, no stertorous breath came out of the darkness, and from under the lamp in front of the
operator only the sounder clicked, always talking,
talking, talking — talking queer things to Russian
ears.

So Chris drew his cap a little lower, for so he always
began, pulled mechanically from his pocket a time-
table, tore off a strip, and holding it carefully open,
sprinkled a few clippings of tobacco upon it, and
rolled his cigarette. He tucked it between his lips;
it was company for the silence, and he could more
easily stop the listening. But he did not light;
only pulled his cap again a little lower, buttoned
close his reefer, looked at his bandaged foot, picked
up his lamp, and started home.

It was dark, and the wind from the north was bitter,
but he made a great detour into the teeth of it —
around by the coal chutes, a long way round, a long

way from the frog of the east house-track switch; and
the cold stung his face as he limped heavily on.   At
last by the ice house he turned south, and reaching
the face of the bench paused a moment, hesitating,
on the side of the earthen stairs; it was very dark.
After a bit he walked slowly down and pushed open
the door of his dugout.   It was dark inside, and
cold; the fire was out.   The children were asleep;
the woman was asleep.

He sat down in a chair and put out his lamp.
There was no Christmas that night in Little Russia.

Cooney

Held for Orders

The Wiper's Story

HOW McGRATH GOT
AN ENGINE

The Wiper's Story

❧

HOW McGRATH GOT
AN ENGINE

THIS came about through there being whiskers on the rails. It may not be generally understood that whiskers grow on steel rails; curious as it seems, they do. Moreover, on steel rails they are dangerous, and, at times, exceedingly dangerous.

Do not infer that all steel rails grow whiskers; nor is it, as one might suppose, only the old rails that sport them. The youngest rail on the curve may boast as stout a beard as the oldest rail on the tangent, and one just as gray. They flourish, too, in spite of orders; for while whiskers are permitted on engineers and tolerated on conductors, they are never encouraged on rails. Nature, however, provides the whiskers, regardless of discipline, and, what is more, shaves them herself.

Their culture depends on conditions. Some months grow better whiskers than others : September is famous for whiskers, while July grows very few. Whiskers will grow on steel rails in the air of a single night ; but not every night air will produce whiskers. It takes a high, frosty air, one that stays out late, to make whiskers. Take, for example, the night air of the Black Hills ; it is known everywhere among steel rails as a beard tonic. The day's moisture, falling as the sun drops beyond the hills is drawn into feathery, jewelled crystals of frost on the chilly steel, as a glass of ice-water beads in summer shade ; and these dewy stalagmites rise in a dainty profusion, until when day peeps into the cañons the track looks like a pair of long white streamers winding up and down the levels. But beware that track. It is a very dangerous track, and its possibilities lie where Samson's lay — in the whiskers.

So it lies in early morning, as pretty a death-trap as any flower that ever lured a fly; only, this pitfall

waits for engines and trains and men — and sometimes gets them.

It waits there on the mountain grades, in an
ambush really deadly for an unwary train, until the
sun, which is particularly lazy in the fall, peeping
over into the cuts, smiles, at length, on the bearded
steel as if it were too funny, and the whiskers
vanish into thin air.

A smooth-faced rail presents no especial dangers;
and if trainmen in the Hills had their way, they would
never turn a wheel until the sun had done barbering.
But despatchers not having to do with them take no
account of whiskers. They make only the schedules,
and the whiskers make the trouble. To lessen their
dangers, engineers always start, up hill or down, with
a tankful of sand, and they sand the whiskers. It is
rough barbering, but it helps the driver-tires grit a bit
into the face of the rail, and in that way hang on. In
this emergency a tankful of sand is better than all the
air Westinghouse ever stored.

Aloysius McGrath was a little sweeper; but he
was an aspiring one, for even a sweeper may aspire,

and in point of fact most of them do aspire. Aloysius
worked in the roundhouse at the head of the Wind
River pass on the West End Mountains.   It is an
amazingly rough country ; and as for grades, it takes
your breath merely to look down the levels. Three
per cent, four per cent, five per cent — it is really
frightful ! But Aloysius was used to heavy falls ; he
had begun working for the company as a sweeper
under Johnnie Horigan, and no engineer would have
thought of running a grade to compare with Johnnie's headers.

Horigan was the first boss Aloysius ever had.
Now Aloysius, if caught just right, is a very pretty
name, but Johnnie Horigan could make nothing whatever of it, so he called Aloysius, Cooney, as he said,
for short — Cooney McGrath — and, by the way, if
you will call that McGraw, we shall be started right.
As for Horigan, he may be called anything ; at least
it is certain that on the West End he has been called
everything.

Johnnie was ordinarily boss sweeper.   He had
suffered numerous promotions — several times to

wiper, and once to hostler; but his tendency to celebrate these occasions usually cost him his job, and he reverted to sweeping. If he had not been such an inoffensive, sawed-off little old nubbin he would n't have been tolerated on the pay rolls; but he had been with the company so long and discharged so often that foremen grew tired of trying to get rid of him, and in spite of his very regular habits, he was hanging on somewhere all the time.

When Johnnie was gone, using the word in at least two senses, Aloysius Cooney McGrath became, *ipso facto*, boss sweeper. It happened first one Sunday morning, just after pay day, when Johnnie applied to the foreman for permission to go to church. Permission was granted, and Johnnie started for church; but it is doubtful whether he ever found it. At all events, at the end of three weeks he turned up again at the roundhouse, considerably the worse for his attempt to locate the house of prayer — which he had tried to find only after he had been kicked out of every other place in town.

Aloysius had improved the interval by sweeping

the roundhouse as it never had been swept before; and
when Johnnie Horigan returned, morally disfigured,
Aloysius McGrath was already promoted to be wiper
over his old superior. Johnnie was in no wise en-
vious. His only move was to turn the misfortune to
account for an ulterior purpose, and he congratulated
the boy, affecting that he had stayed away to let them
see what stuff the young fellow was made of. This
put him in a position to negotiate a small loan from
his *protégé* — a position of which he never neglected
the possibilities. It was out of the question to be mad
very long at Johnnie, though one might be very often.
After a time Aloysius got to firing : then he wanted
an engine.   But he fired many months, and there
came no promotion.   The trouble was, there were
no new crews added to the engine service. Nobody
got killed ; nobody quit ; nobody died.   One, two,
and three years without a break, and little Aloysius
had become a bigger Aloysius, and was still firing ;
he became also discouraged, for then the force was
cut down and he was put back wiping.

"Never y' mind, never y' mind, Cooney," old

Johnnie would say. " It 'll come all right. You 'll
get y'r ingin' yet.   Lind me a couple till pay-a-day,
Cooney, will you ?   I 'll wahrant y' y'r ingin' yet,
Cooney."   Which little assurance always cost
Aloysius two dollars till pay day, and no end of
trouble getting it back ; for when he attempted collection, Johnnie took a very dark view of the lad's
future, alluding vaguely to people who were hard-
hearted and ungrateful to their best friends.   And
though Aloysius paid slight attention to the old
sweeper's vaporings, he really was in the end the
means of the boy's getting his engine.

After three years of panic and hard times on the
mountain division, the mines began to reopen, new
spurs were laid out, construction crews were put on,
and a new activity was everywhere apparent.   But to
fill the cup of Aloysius' woe, the new crews were all
sent up from McCloud.   That they were older men
in the order of promotion was cold comfort — Aloysius felt crowded out.   He went very blue, and the
next time Johnnie applied for a loan Aloysius rebuffed
him unfeelingly ; this in turn depressed John.

" Never mind, never mind, Cooney.　I 'll not be speakin' t' Neighbor agin t' set y' up.　If y' like wipin', stick to ut.　I 'll not be troublin' Neighbor agin."　Johnnie professed a great pull with the master mechanic.

That Aloysius might feel still more the sting of his coldness, Johnnie for some days paid much court to the new firemen and engine runners.　Nothing about the house was too good for them, and as the crafty sweeper never overlooked an opportunity, he was in debt before the end of the week to most of the brotherhood.

But the memorable morning for Aloysius came shortly thereafter.　It was one of those keen October mornings that bite so in the Hills.　The construction train, Extra 240 West, had started about five o'clock from the head of the pass with a load of steel for the track layers, and stopped for a bite of breakfast at Wind River.　Above the roundhouse there is a switchback.　When the train pulled in, the crew got off for some hot coffee.　Johnnie Horigan was around playing good fellow, and he climbed into the cab to

run the train through the switchback while the crews
were at the eating house. It was irregular to leave
the engine, but they did, and as for Johnnie Horigan,
he was regularly irregular. There were sixteen cars
of steel in the string, besides a cabooseful of laborers.
The backing up the leg of the nipper was easy. After
the switch was newly set, Johnnie pulled down the
lower leg ; and that, considering the whiskers, was
too easy.

When he pulled past the eating house on the down
grade, he was going so lively with his flats that he
was away before the crew could get out of the lunch
room. In just one minute everybody in Wind
River was in trouble : the crew, because their
train was disappearing down the cañon ; the eating
house man, because nobody paid him for his coffee ;
and Johnnie Horigan, because he found it impossible to stop. He had dumped the sand, he had
applied the air, he had reversed the engine — by all
the rules laid down in the instruction car she ought
to stop. But she did n't stop, and — this was the
embarrassing feature — she was headed down a hill

twenty miles long, with curves to weary a boa-constrictor. John hung his head wildly over the drivers, looked back at the yelling crew, contemplated the load that was pushing him down the grade and his head began to swim. There appeared but one thing more to do: that was to make a noise; and as he neared the roundhouse he whistled like the wind. Aloysius O'Cooney McGrath, at the alarm, darted out of the house like a fox. As he reached the door he saw the construction train coming, and Johnnie Horigan in the gangway looking for a soft place to light.

The wiper chartered the situation in a mental second. The train was running away, and Horigan was leaving it to its fate. From any point of view it was a tough proposition, but tough propositions come rarely to ambitious railroad men, and Aloysius was starving for any sort of a proposition that would help him out of the waste. The laborers in the caboose, already bewildered, were craning anxiously from the windows. Horigan, opposite the roundhouse, jumped in a sprawl; the engine was shot past Aloysius; boarding was out of the question.

But on the siding stood a couple of flats, empty; and with his hair straight on centres, the little wiper ran for them and mounted the nearest. The steel train was jumping. Aloysius, bunching his muscle, ran the length of the two flats for a head, and, from the far corner, threw himself across the gap, like a bat, on a load of the runaway steel. Scrambling to his feet, he motioned and yelled to the hoboes, who were pouring frantic out on the hind flat of the string, to set brakes; then he made ahead for the engine.

It was a race with the odds all wrong, for with every yard Aloysius gained, the train gained a dozen. By the time he reached the tender, breathless, and slid down the coal into the deserted cab, the train was heading into Little Horn gap, and every Italian aboard, yelling for life. Aloysius jumped into the levers, poked his head through the window, and looked at the drivers. They were in the back motion, and in front of them the sand was stream-

ing wide open. The first thing he did was to
shut half it off — the fight could not be won by
wasting ammunition. Over and over again he
jerked at the air. It was refusing its work. Where
so many a hunted runner has turned for salvation
there was none for Aloysius. He opened and
closed, threw on and threw off; it was all one,
and all useless. The situation was as simple as it
was frightful. Even if they did n't leave the track,
they were certain to smash into Number Sixteen,
the up-passenger, which must meet them somewhere on the hill.

Aloysius's fingers closed slowly on the sand lever.
There was nothing on earth for it but sand, merely
sand; and even the wiper's was oozing with the
stream that poured from the tank on the whiskered
rails. He shut off a bit more, thinking of the terrific curves below, and mentally calculated — or tried
to — how long his steam would last to reverse the
drivers — how he could shovel coal and sand the
curves at the same time — and how much slewing
the Italians at the tail of the kite could stand without landing on the rocks.

The pace was giddy and worse. When his brain was whirling fastest, a man put a hand on his shoulder. Aloysius started as if Davy Jones had tapped him, and between bounces looked, scared, around. He looked into a face he did n't know from Adam's, but there was sand in the eyes that met his.

" What can I do ? "

Aloysius saw the man's lips move, and, without taking his hands from the levers, bent his head to catch the words.

" What can I do ? " shouted the man at his elbow.

" Give me steam — steam," cried the wiper, looking straight ahead.

It was the foreman of the steel gang from the caboose. Aloysius, through the backs of his eyes, saw him grab the shovel and make a pass at the tender. Doing so, he nearly took a header through the gangway, but he hung to the shovel and braced himself better.

With the next attempt he got a shovelful into the cab, but in the delivery passed it well up Aloysius's

neck. There were neither words nor grins, but
just another shovelful of coal a minute after; and
the track-layer, in spite of the dizzy lurching, shot
it where it belonged — into the furnace. Feeling
that if one shovelful could be landed, more could,
Alyosius's own steam rose. As they headed madly
around the Cinnamon bend the dial began to climb
in spite of the obstacles; and the wiper, considering there were two, and the steam and the sand to
fight the thing out, opened his valve and dusted the
whiskers on the curve with something more than a
gleam of hope.

If there was confusion on the runaway train, there
was terror and more below it. As the spectre flitted
past Pringle station, five miles down the valley, the
agent caught a glimpse of the sallow face of the
wiper at the cab window, and saw the drivers whirling backward. He rushed to his key and called the
Medicine Bend despatcher. With a tattoo like a
drum-roll the despatcher in turn called Soda Springs,
ten miles below Pringle, where Number Sixteen, the
up-passenger, was then due. He rattled on with

his heart in his fingers, and answer came on the
instant.   Then an order flashed into Soda Springs:

To No. 16.
Take Soda Springs siding quick.   Extra 240
West has lost control of the train.   Di.

There never was such a bubbling at Soda Springs
as that bubbling.   The operator tore up the platform
like a hawk in a chicken yard.   Men never scattered so quick as when Number Sixteen began
screaming and wheezing and backing for the clear.
Above the town, Aloysius, eyes white to the sockets,
shooting the curves like a meteor, watched his less-
ening stream of sand pour into the frost on the track.
As they whipped over bridges and fills the caboose
reeled like a dying top — fear froze every soul on
board.   To leave the track now meant a scatter
that would break West End records.

When Soda Springs sighted Extra 240 West, pitch-
ing down the mountain, the steel dancing behind and
Aloysius jumping before, there was a painful sensation — the sensation of good men who see a disaster

they are powerless to avert.   Nor did Soda Springs
know how desperate the wiper's extremity had become.   Not even the struggling steel foreman knew
that with Soda Springs passing like the films of a
cinematograph, and two more miles of down-grade
ahead, the last cupful of sand was trickling from the
wiper's tank.   Aloysius, at that moment, would n't
have given the odd change on a pay check for all the
chances Extra 240 and he himself had left. He stuck
to his levers merely because there was no particular
reason for letting go.   It was only a question of how
a man wanted to take the rocks.   Yet, with all his
figuring, Aloysius had lost sight of his only salvation
— maybe because it was quite out of his power to
effect it himself.   But in making the run up to Soda
Springs Number Sixteen had already sanded the rails
below.

He could feel the help the minute the tires ground
into the grit.   They began to smoke, and Aloysius
perceived the grade was easing somewhat.   Even
the dazed foreman, looking back, saw an improvement in the lurch of the caboose.   There was one

more hair-raiser ahead — the appalling curve at the
forks of the Goose. But, instead of being hurled
over the elevation, they found themselves around it
and on the bridge with only a vicious slew. Aloysius's hair began to lie down, and his heart to
rise up. He had her checked — even the hoboes
knew it — and a mile further, with the dangers
past, they took new ones by dropping off the hind
end.

At the second bend below the Goose, Aloysius
made a stop, and began again to breathe. A box was
blazing on the tender truck, and, with his handy
fireman, he got down at once to doctor it. The
whole thing shifted so mortally quick from danger
to safety that the two never stopped to inventory
their fears ; they seemed to have vanished with the
frost that lured them to destruction. They jumped
together into the cab ; and whistling at the laborers strung back along the right of way Extra 240
West began backing pluckily up hill to Soda Springs.
The first man who approached the cab as they slowed
down for the platform — in fact, people rather stood

back for him — was Bucks, Superintendent of the Division ; his car had come in attached to Number Sixteen.

"How did your train get away from you ? " he asked of Aloysius; there was neither speculation nor sympathy in his manner and his words were bitten with frost.

" It did n't get away from me," retorted Aloysius, who had never before in his life seen the man, and was not aware that he owed him any money.   But the operator at the Springs, who knew Aloysius and the superintendent both, was standing behind the latter doing a pantomime that would shame a medicine man.

" Quick talking will do more for you than smart talking," replied the superintendent, crisply. "You'll never get a better chance while you 're working for this company to explain yourself."

Aloysius himself began to think so, for the nods and winks of the operator were bewildering. He tried to speak up, but the foreman of the steel gang put in : "See here, sport," he snapped, irreverently, at the angry official. "Why don't you cool your hat before you jump a fellow like that?"

"What business is it of yours how I jump a fellow?" returned the superintendent, sharply, "who are you?"

"I'm only foreman of this steel gang, my friend; and I don't take any back talk from anybody."

"In that case," responded Bucks, with velvet sarcasm, "perhaps *you* will explain things. I'm only superintendent of this division; but it's customary to inquire into matters of this kind."

Aloysius at the words nearly sank to the platform; but the master of the hoboes, who had all the facts, went at the big man as if he had been one of the gang, and did not falter till he had covered the perspiring wiper with glory.

"What's the reason the air would n't work?" asked the superintendent, turning, without comment, when the track-layer had finished, to Aloysius.

"I have n't had time to find out, sir."

"Find out and report to me. What's your name?"

" McGrath."

" McGraw, eh ? Well, McGraw, look close into the air. There may be something in it for you. You did the firing ? " he added, turning short again on the unabashed steel foreman.

" What there was done."

" I 'll do a little now myself. I 'll fire you right here and now for impertinence."

" I suppose you 're the boss," responded the man of ties, imperturbably. " When I made the crack, I 'd made it harder if I had known who you were."

" You know now, don't you ? "

" I guess so."

" Very good," said Bucks, in his mildest tones. " If you will report to me at Medicine Bend this afternoon, I 'll see whether we can't find something better for your manners than cursing hoboes. You can ride down in my car, sport. What do you say ? That will save you transportation."

It brought a yell from the railroad men crowding around, for that was Bucks's way of doing things ; and the men liked Bucks and his way. The ex-captain of the dagoes tried to look cool, but in point of fact went very sheepish at his honors.

Followed by a mob, eager to see the finish, Superintendent Bucks made his way up the track along the construction train to where Aloysius and the engineer of Number Sixteen were examining the air. They found it frozen between the first and the second car. Bucks heard it all — heard the whole story. Then he turned to his clerk.

"Discharge both crews of Extra 240. Fire Johnnie Horigan."

"Yes, sir."

"McGrath, run your train back to Wind River behind us. We'll scare up a conductor here somewhere; if we can't, I'll be your conductor. Make your report to Medicine Bend," Bucks added, speaking to the operator; and without further words walked back to his car.

As he turned away, the engineer of Number Sixteen slapped Aloysius on the back:

"Kid, why the blazes did n't you thank him?"

"Who?"

" Bucks."

" What for? "

" What for? Jiminey Christmas! What for? Did n't he just make you an engineer? Did n't he just say, 'Run your train back behind us to Wind River'? "

" My train? "

" Sure, your train. Do you think Bucks ever says a thing like that without meaning it? You bet not."

Bucks's clerk, too, was a little uncertain about the promotion. " I suppose he 's competent to run the train back, is n't he? " he asked of Bucks, suggestively.

Bucks was scrawling a message.

" A man that could hold a train from Wind River here on whiskers, with nothing but a tankful of sand and a hobo fireman, would n't be likely to fall off the right of way running back," he returned dryly. " He 's been firing for years, has n't he? We have n't got half enough men like McGraw. Tell Neighbor to give him an engine."

Hailey

Held for Orders

The Roadmaster's Story

THE SPIDER WATER

The Roadmaster's Story

THE SPIDER WATER

NOT officially; I don't pretend to say that. You might travel the West End from fresh water to salt — and we dip into both — without ever locating the Spider Water by map or by name.

But if you should happen anywhere on the West End to sit among a gang of bridge carpenters; or get to confidence with a bridge foreman; or find the springy side of a roadmaster's heart; *then*, you might hear all you wanted about the Spider Water — maybe more; anyway, full plenty, as Hailey used to say.

The Sioux named it; and whatever may be thought of their interpretation of Scriptural views on land-grabbing, no man with sense ever attempted to improve on their names for things, whether birds, or braves, or winds, or waters — they know.

Our General Managers had n't always sense — this may seem odd, but on the system it would excite no comment — and one of them countenanced a shameful change in the name of the Spider Water. Some polytechnical idiot at a safe distance dubbed it The Big Sandy ; and the Big Sandy it is to this day on map and in folder — but not in the lingo of trackmen nor the heart of the Sioux. Don't say Big Sandy to trackmen and hand out a cigar. It will not go. Say Spider Water without any cigar and you will get a word and a stool, and if you ask it, fine cut.

The Spider Water — although ours is the pioneer line — was there when we first bridged it. It is probably as old as sundown, and nothing like as pretty. The banks — it has none to speak of. Its stones — they are whiskered. Its bed — full of sand-burs. Everything about the villain stream has a dilapidate, broken-down air : the very mud of the Spider Water is rusty.

So our people bridged it; and the trouble began. A number of matters bothered our pioneer managements — Indians, outlaws, cabinet officers, congressional committees, and Wall Street magnates — but at one time or another our folks managed all of them. The only thing they could n't at any time satisfactorily manage was the Spider Water. Bridge after bridge they threw across it — and into it. Year after year the Spider Water toyed with our civil engineers and our material department. One man at Omaha given to asthma and statistics estimated, between spells, that the Spider Water had cost us more money than all the water courses together from the Missouri to the Sierras.

Then came to the West End a masterful man, a Scotchman, pawky and hard. Brodie was his name, an Edinburgh man with no end of degrees and master of every one. Brodie came to be superintendent of bridges on the Western Division, and to boss every water course on the plains and in the mountains. But the Spider Water took a fall even out of Brodie. It swept out a Howe

truss bridge for Brodie before he got his bag un-
packed, and thereafter Brodie, who was reputed not
to care a stringer for anybody, did not conceal a
distinct respect for the Spider.

Brodie went at it right.   He tried, not to make
friends with the Spider, for nobody could do that,
but to get acquainted with it.   For this he went
to its oldest neighbors, the Sioux.   Brodie spent
weeks and weeks up the Spider Water hunting,
summers; and with the Sioux he talked Spider
Water and drank fire-water.   That was Brodie's
shame — the fire-water.

But he was pawky, and he chinned unceasingly
the braves and the medicine men about the uncom-
monly queer water that took the bridges so fast.
The river that month in and month out could n't
squeeze up water enough to baptize a pollywog
and then, of a sudden, and for a few days, would
rage like the Missouri, restore to the desert its own
and living image, and leave our bewildered rails
hung up either side in the wind.

Brodie talked cloudbursts up country; for the

floods came, times, under clear skies — and the
Sioux sulked in silence.   He suggested an unsus-
pected inlet from some mountain stream which
maybe, times, sent its storm water over a low
divide into the Spider — and the red men shrugged
their faces.   As a last resort and in desperation he
hinted at the devil; and the sceptics took a quick
brace with as much as to say, now you *are* talking;
and muttered very bad Medicine.

Then they gave him the Indian stuff about the
Spider Water; took him away up where once a
party of Pawnees had camped in the dust of the
river bed to surprise the Sioux; and told Brodie
how the Spider, more sudden than buck, fleeter
than pony, had come down in the night and surprised the Pawnees — and so well that the next
morning there was n't enough material left for a
scalp dance.

They took Brodie out into the ratty bed himself
and when he said, heap dry, and said, no water,
they laughed, Indianwise, and pointed to the sand.
Scooping little wells with their hands they showed

him the rising and the filling; the instant water
where before was no water. And dropping into
the wells feathers of the grouse, they showed Brodie how the current carried them always across the
well — every time, and always, Brodie noticed —
southeast. Then Brodie made Hailey dig many
holes, and the Spider welled into them, and he
threw in bits of notebooks and tobacco wrappers,
but always they travelled southeast — always the
same; and a bigger fool than Brodie could see
that the water was all there, only underground.
But when did it rise? asked Brodie. When the
Chinook spoke, said the Sioux. And why? persisted Brodie. Because the Spider woke, said the
Sioux. And Brodie went out of the camp of the
Sioux wondering.

And he planned a new bridge which should stand
the Chinook and the Spider and the de'il himself,
said Brodie, Medicine or no Medicine. And full
seven year it lasted; then the fire-water spoke for
the wicked Scotchman — and he himself went out
into the night.

And after he died, miserable wreck of a man —
and of a very great man — the Spider woke and
took his pawky bridge and tied up the main line
for two weeks and set us crazy — for we were
already losing our grip on the California fast freight
business. But at that time Hailey was superintendent of bridges on the West End.

I

HIS father was a section foreman. When
Hailey was a kid — a mere kid — he
got into Brodie's office doing errands;
but whenever he saw a draughtsman at work he was
no good for errands. At such times he went all
into a mental tangle that could neither be thrashed
nor kicked out of him, though both were conscien-
tiously tried by old man Hailey and Superintendent
Brodie; and Brodie, since he could do nothing else
with him, finally kicked him into learning to read —
and to cipher, Brodie called it. Then, by and by,
Hailey got an old table and part of a cake of India ink

himself, and himself became a draughtsman, and soon, with some cursing from Brodie and a "Luk a' that now!" from his paralyzed daddy, became chief draughtsman in Brodie's office.   Hailey was no college man — Hailey was a Brodie man.   Single mind on single mind — concentration absolute.   Mathematics, drawing, bridges, brains — that was Hailey. But no classics except Brodie, who himself was a classic.   All that Brodie knew, Hailey had from him; and where Brodie was weak, Hailey was strong — master of himself.   When Brodie shamed the image he was made in, Hailey hid the shame best he could, — though never touched or made it his own — and Brodie, who hated even himself, showed still a light in the wreck by molding Hailey to his work.   For, one day, said Brodie in his heart, this boy shall be master of these bridges.   When I am rot, he will be here what I ought to have been — this Irish boy — and they will say he was Brodie's man.   And better than any of these dough-heads they send me out, better than any of their Eastern graduates he shall be, if he was made engineer by a drunkard.   And

Hailey was better, far, far better than the graduates, better than Brodie — and to Hailey came the time to wrestle the Spider.

Stronger than any man before or since he was for that work. All Brodie knew, all the Indians knew, all that a life's experience, eating, living, watching, sleeping with the big river had taught him, that Hailey knew. And when Brodie's bridge went out, Hailey was ready with his new bridge for the Spider Water which should be better than Brodie's, just as he was better than Brodie. It was to be such a bridge as Brodie's bridge with the fire-water left out. And the plans for a Howe truss, two pier, two abutment, three span, pneumatic caisson bridge to span the Big Sandy River were submitted to headquarters.

But the cost! The directors jumped their table when they saw the figures. We were being milked at that time — to put it bluntly, being sucked, worse than lemons — by a Wall Street clique that robbed our good road, shaved our salaries, impoverished our equipment, and cut our maintenance to the quick. They talked economy and studied piracy. In the matter of appropriations, for themselves they were free-booters; for us, they were thrifty as men of Hamelin town. When Hailey demanded a thousand guilders for his Spider Water bridge, they laughed and said, "Come, take fifty." He could n't do anything else; and he built a fifty guilder bridge to bar the Spider's crawl. It lasted really better than the average bridge and since Hailey never could get a thousand guilders at once, he kept drawing fifty at a time and throwing them annually at the Spider.

But the dream of his life — this *we* all knew, and the Sioux would have said the Spider knew — was to build a final bridge over the Spider Water: a bridge to throttle it for all time.

It was the one subject on which you could get a rise out of Hailey any time, day or night, — the two pier, two abutment, three span, pneumatic caisson Spider bridge. He would talk Spider bridge to a Chinaman. His bridge foreman Ed Peeto, a staving big, one-eyed French Canadian, actually had but two ideas in life: one was Hailey; the other the Spider bridge. When the management changed again —

when the pirates were sent out on the plank so many good men had walked at their command — and a great and public-spirited man took control of the system, Ed Peeto kicked his little water spaniel in a frenzy of delight. "Now, Sport, old boy," he exclaimed riotously, "we'll get the bridge!"

So there were many long conferences at division headquarters between Bucks, superintendent, and Callahan, assistant, and Hailey, superintendent of bridges, and after, Hailey went once more to general headquarters lugging all his estimates revised and all his plans refigured. All his expense estimates outside the Spider bridge and one other point were slight, because Hailey could skin along with less money than anybody ever in charge of the bridge work. He did it by keeping everything up; not a sleeper, not a spike — nothing got away from him.

The new president, as befitted a very big man, was no end of a swell, and received Hailey with a considerate dignity unknown on our End. He listened carefully to the superintendent's statement of the necessities at the Big Sandy River. The amount

looked large ; but the argument, supported by a mass
of statistics, was convincing.   Three bridges in ten
years, and the California fast freight business lost
twice.   Hailey's budget called, too, for a new bridge
at the Peace River — and a good one.   Give him
these, he said in effect, and he would guarantee the
worst stretch on the system for a lifetime against tie-
up disasters.   Hailey stayed over to await the decision ; but he was always in a hurry, and he haunted
the general offices until the president told him he
could have the money.   To Hailey this meant, particularly, the bridge of his dreams.   The wire flashed
the word to the West End; everybody at the Wickiup
was glad ; but Ed Peeto burned red fire and his little
dog Sport ate rattlesnakes.

The old shack of a depot building that served as
division headquarters at Medicine Bend we called
the Wickiup.   Everybody in it was crowded for
room, and Hailey, whose share was what was left,
had hard work to keep out of the wastebasket.   But
right away now it was different.   Two extra offices
were assigned to Hailey, and he took his place with

those who sported windows and cuspidors — in a word, had departments in the service.   Old Denis Hailey went very near crazy. He resigned as section boss and took a place at smaller wages in the bridge carpenter's gang so he could work on the boy's bridge, and Ed Peeto, savage with responsibility, strutted around the Wickiup like a cyclops.

For a wonder the bridge material came in fast — the Spider stuff first — and early in the summer Hailey, very quiet, and Peeto, very profane, with all and several their traps and slaves and belongings moved into construction headquarters at the Spider, and the first airlock ever sunk west of the Missouri closed over the heads of tall Hailey and big Ed Peeto.   Like a swarm of ants the bridge-workers cast the refuse up out of the Spider bed.   The blow-pipes never slept: night and day the sand streamed from below, and Hailey's caissons, like armed cruisers, sunk foot by foot towards the rock; by the middle of September the masonry was crowding high-water mark, and the following Saturday Hailey and Peeto ran back to Medicine

Bend to rest up a bit and get acquainted with their families. Peeto was so deaf he could n't hear himself swear, and Hailey looked ragged and thin, like the old depot, but immensely happy.

Sunday morning counted a little even then in the mountains. It was at least a day to get your feet on the tables up in Bucks's office and smoke Callahan's Cavendish — which was enough to make a man bless Callahan if he did forget his Maker. Sunday mornings Bucks would get out the dainty, pearl-handled Wostenholm that Lillienfeld, the big San Francisco spirit-shipper, left annually for him at the Bend, and open the R. R. B. mail and read the news aloud for the benefit of Callahan and Hailey and such hangers-on as Peeto and an occasional stray despatcher.

" Hello," exclaimed Bucks, chucking a nine-inch official manila under the table, " here 's a general order — Number Fourteen —— "

The boys drew their briers like one. Bucks read out a lot of stuff that did n't touch our End, and then he reached this paragraph :

" ' The Mountain and the Inter-mountain divisions are hereby consolidated under the name of the Mountain Division with J. F. Bucks as Superintendent, headquarters at Medicine Bend. C. T. Callahan is appointed Assistant Superintendent of the new division.' "

" Good boy ! " roared Ed Peeto, straining his ears.

"Well, well, well," said Hailey, opening his eyes, " here 's promotions right and left."

" ' H. P. Agnew is appointed Superintendent of bridges of the new division with headquarters at Omaha, vice P. C. Hailey,' " Bucks read on, with some little surprise growing into a shock. Then he read fast looking for some further mention of Hailey. Hailey promoted, transferred, assigned — but there was no further mention of Hailey in G. O. Number Fourteen. Bucks threw down the order in a silence. Ed Peeto broke out first.

" Who 's H. P. Canoe ? "

" Agnew."

" Who the hell is he ? " roared Ed. Nobody answered : nobody knew. Bucks attempted to talk ;

Callahan lit his lighted pipe; but Ed Peeto stared at Hailey like a drunken man.

" Did you hear that? " he snorted at his superior. Hailey nodded.

" You 're out! " stormed Peeto.

Hailey nodded. The bridge foreman took his pipe from his mouth and dashed it into the stove. He got up and stamped across to the window and was like to have sworn the glass out before Hailey spoke.

" I 'm glad we 're up to high water at the Spider, Bucks," said he at last. " When they get in the Peace River work, the division will run itself for a year."

" Hailey," Bucks spoke slowly, " I don't need to tell you what I think of it, do I? It 's a damned shame. But it 's what I 've said for a year — nobody ever knows what Omaha will do next."

Hailey rose to his feet. " Where you going, Phil? " asked Bucks.

" Going back to the Spider on Number Two."

" Not going back this morning — why don't you wait for Four, to-night? " suggested Bucks.

"Ed," Hailey raised his voice at the foreman, "will you get those stay-bolts and chuck them into the baggage-car for me on Number Two? I'm going over to the house for a minute." He forgot to answer Bucks; they knew what it meant. He was bracing himself to tell the folks before he left them. Preparing to explain why he wouldn't have the Sunday at home with the children. Preparing to tell the wife — and the old man — that he was out. Out of the railroad system he had given his life to help build up and make what it was. Out of the position he had climbed to by studying like a hermit and working like a hobo. Out — without criticism, or allegation, or reason — simply, like a dog, out.

Nobody at the Wickiup wanted to hear the telling over at the cottage; nobody wanted to imagine the scene. As Number Two's mellow chime whistle rolled down the gorge, they saw Hailey coming out of his house, his wife looking after him, and two little girls tugging at his arms as he hurried along; old Denis behind, head down, carrying the boy's shabby valise, trying to understand why the blow had fallen.

That was what Callahan up with Bucks at the window was trying to figure — what it meant.

"The man that looks to Omaha for rhyme or reason will beggar his wits, Callahan," said Bucks slowly, as he watched Ed Peeto swing the stay-bolts up into the car so they would crack the baggageman across the shins, and then try to get him into a fight about it. "They never had a man — and I bar none, no, not Brodie — that could handle the mountain-water like Hailey; they never will have a man — and they dump him out like a pipe of tobacco. How does it happen we are cursed with such a crew of blooming idiots? Other roads are n't."

Callahan made no answer. "I know why they did it," Bucks went on, "but I could n't tell Hailey."

" Why? "

" I think I know why. Last time I was down, the president brought his name up and asked a lot of questions about where he was educated and so on. Somebody had plugged him, I could see that in two minutes. I gave him the facts — told him that Brodie had given him his education as an engineer. The minute he found out he was n't regularly graduated, he froze up. Very polite, but he froze up. See? Experience, actual acquirements," Bucks extended his hand from his vest pocket in an odd wavy motion till it was lost at arm's length, " nothing — nothing — nothing."

As he concluded, Hailey was climbing behind his father into the smoker; Number Two pulled down the yard and out; one thing Hailey meant to make sure of — that they should n't beat him out of the finish of the Spider bridge as he had planned it; one monument Hailey meant to have — one he has.

The new superintendent of bridges took hold promptly; we knew he had been wired for long before his appointment was announced. He was a good enough fellow, I guess, but we all hated him. Bucks did the civil, though, and took Agnew down to the Spider in a special to inspect the new work and introduce him to the man whose bread and opportunity he was taking. "I've been wanting to meet you, Mr. Hailey," said Agnew pleasantly after they had shaken hands. Hailey looked at Agnew silently as he spoke; Bucks looked steadfastly at the grasshopper derrick.

"I've been expecting you'd be along pretty soon," replied Hailey presently. "There's considerable to look over here. After that we'll go back to Peace River cañon. We're just getting things started there: then we'll run up to the Bend and I'll turn the office over."

"No hurry about that. You've got a good deal of a bridge here, Mr. Hailey?"

"You'll need a good deal of a bridge here."

"I did n't expect to find you so far along out here in the mountains. Where did you get that pneumatic process?"

It touched Hailey, the pleasant, easy way Agnew took him. The courtesy of the east against the blunt of the west. There was n't a mean drop anywhere in Hailey's blood, and he made no trouble whatever for his successor.

After he let go on the West End Hailey talked as if he would look up something further east.   He spoke about it to Bucks, but Bucks told him frankly he would find difficulty without a regular degree in getting a satisfactory connection.   Hailey himself realized that ; moreover, he seemed reluctant to quit the mountains.   He acted around the cottage and the Wickiup like a man who has lost something and who looks for it abstractedly — as one might feel in his pockets for a fishpole or a burglar.   But there were lusty little Haileys over at the cottage to be looked after, and Bucks, losing a roadmaster about that time, asked Hailey (after chewing it a long time with Callahan) to take the place himself and stay on the staff.   He even went home with Hailey and argued it.

" I know it does n't seem just right," Bucks put it, "but, Hailey, you must remember this thing at Omaha is n't going to last.   They can't run a road like this with Harvard graduates and Boston typewriters. There 'll be an entire new deal down there some fine day. Stay here with me, and I 'll say this, Hailey, if I go, ever, you go with me."

And Hailey, sitting with his head between his hands, listening to his wife and to Bucks, said, one day, "Enough," and the first of the month reported for duty as roadmaster.

Agnew, meantime, had stopped all construction work not too far along to discontinue. The bridge at the Spider fortunately was beyond his mandate; it was finished to a rivet as Hailey had planned it. Three spans, two piers, and a pair of abutments — solid as the Tetons. But the Peace River cañon work was caught in the air. Hailey's caissons gave way to piles which pulled the cost down from one hundred to seventy-five thousand dollars, and incidentally it was breathed that the day for extravagant expenditures on the West End was past — and Bucks dipped a bit deeper than usual into Callahan's box of cross-cut, and rammed the splintered leaf into his brier a bit harder and said no word.

" But if we lose just one more bridge it 's good-
bye and gone to the California fast freight business," muttered Callahan.   " It 's taken two years
to get it back as it is.   Did you tell the president
that ? " he growled at Bucks, smoking.   Bucks
put out his little wave.

" I told him everything.   I told him we could n't
stand another tie-up.   I showed them all the records.   One bridge at Peace River, three at the
Spider in ten years."

" What did they say ? "

" Said they had entire confidence in Agnew's
judgment;   very eminent authority and that sort —
new blood was making itself felt in every department ;   that, of course, was fired at me ;   but they
heard all I intended to say, just the same.   I asked
the blooming board whether they wanted my resignation and — "   Bucks paused to laugh silently,
" the president invited me up to the Millard to dine
with him.   Hello, Phil Hailey ! " he exclaimed as
the new roadmaster walked in the door.   " Happy
New Year.   How 's your culverts, old boy ?   Ed

Peeto said yesterday the piles were going in down
at Peace River."

"Just as good as concrete as long as they stay
in," smiled Hailey, " and they do cost a heap less.
This is great bridge weather — and for that matter
great track weather."

We had no winter that year till spring ; and no
spring till summer ; and it was a spring of snow
and a summer of water.   Down below, the plains
were lost in the snow after Easter even, the snow
that brought the Blackwood disaster with three
engines and a rotary to the bad, not to speak of old
man Sankey, a host in himself.   After that the
snow let up ; it was then no longer a matter of
keeping the line clear; it was a matter of lashing
the track to the right of way to keep it from swimming clear.   Hailey had his hands full ; he caught
it all the while and worse than anybody, but he
worked like two men, for in a pinch that was his
way.   Bucks, irritable from repeated blows of for-
tune, leaned on the wiry roadmaster as he did on
Callahan or Neighbor.   Hailey knew Bucks looked

to him for the track and he strained every nerve making ready for the time the mountain snows should go out.

There was nobody easy on the West End : and least of all Hailey, for that spring, ahead of the suns, ahead of the thaws, ahead of the waters, came a going out that unsettled the oldest calculator in the Wickiup. Brodie's old friends began coming out of the upper country, out of the Spider valley. Over the Eagle pass and through the Peace cañon the Sioux came in parties and camps and tribes — out and down and into the open country. And Bucks stayed them and talked with them. Talked the great White Father and the Ghost dance and the Bad Agent. But the Sioux grunted and did not talk ; they traveled. Then Bucks spoke of good hunting, far, far south ; if they were uneasy Bucks was willing they should travel far, for it looked like a rising. Some kind of a rising it must have been to take the Indians out of winter quarters at such a time. After Bucks, Hailey tried, and the braves listened for they knew Hailey and when he accused them of fixing for fight they shook their heads, denied, and turned their faces to the mountains.   They stretched their arms straight out under their blankets like stringers and put out their palms, downward, and muttered to Hailey.

"Plenty snow."

"I reckon they're lying," said Bucks, listening. "There's some deviltry up.   They're not the kind to clear out for snow."

Hailey made no comment. Only looked thoughtfully at the ponies shambling along, the squaws trudging, the braves loitering to ask after the firewater chief who slept under a cairn of stones off the right of way above the yard.   Bucks didn't believe it.   He could fancy rats deserting a sinking ship, because he had read of such things — but Indians clearing out for snow !

"Not for snow, nor for water," muttered Bucks, "unless it's fire-water."   And once more the red man was misunderstood.

Now the Spider wakes regularly twice ; at all other times irregularly.   Once in April ; that is

the foothills water: once in June; that is the mountain water.   And the June rise is like this⌒.
But the April rise is like this —⌒—.

Now came an April without any rise; that April
nothing rose — except the snow.   "We shall get
it all together," suggested Bucks one night.

"Or will it get us altogether?" asked Hailey.

"Either way," said Callahan, "it will be mostly
at once."

May opened bleaker than April; even the trackmen walked with set faces; the dirtiest half-breed
on the line knew now what the mountains held.
At last, while we looked and wondered, came a very
late Chinook; July in May; then the water.

II

SECTION gangs were doubled and track-
walkers put on. By-passes were opened,
bridge crews strengthened, everything
buckled for grief.   Gullies began to race, culverts to
choke, creeks to tumble, rivers to madden.   From the

Muddy to the Summit the water courses swelled and boiled — all but the Spider; the big river slept. Through May and into June the Spider slept; but Hailey was there at the Wickiup, always, and with one eye running over all the line, one eye turned always to the Spider where two men and two, night and day, watched the lazy surface water trickle over and through the vagabond bed between Hailey's monumental piers.   Never an hour did the operating department lose to the track.   East and west of us railroads everywhere clamored in despair. The flood reached from the Rockies to the Alleghenies.   Our trains never missed a trip; our schedules were unbroken; our people laughed; we got the business, dead loads of it; our treasury flowed over; and Hailey watched; and the Spider slept.

Big Ed Peeto, still foreman of the bridges, hung on Hailey's steps and tried with his staring, swearing eye to make it all out; to guess what Hailey expected to happen, for it was plain he was thinking.   Whether smoking or speaking, whether wak-

ing or sleeping, he was thinking. And as May turned
soft and hot into June with every ditch bellying and
the mountains still buried, it put us all thinking.

On the 30th there was trouble beyond Wild Hat
and all our extra men, put out there under Hailey,
were fighting to hold the Rat valley levels where
they hug the river on the west slope. It was n't
really Hailey's track. Bucks sent him over there
because he sent Hailey wherever the Emperor sent
Ney. Sunday while Hailey was at Wild Hat it
began raining. Sunday it rained. Monday it
rained all through the mountains; Tuesday it was
raining from Omaha to Eagle pass, with the ther-
mometer climbing for breath and the barometer
flat as an adder — and the Spider woke.

Woke with the April water and the June water
and the rain water all at once. Trackmen at the
bridge Tuesday night flagged Number One and reported the river wild, and sheet ice running. A
wire from Bucks brought Hailey out of the west
and into the east; and brought him to reckon for
the last time with his ancient enemy.

He was against it Wednesday morning with dyna-
mite.   All the day, the night and the next day the
sullen roar of the giant powder shook the ice-jams.
Two days more he spent there watching, with only
an occasional thunderbolt to heave and scatter the
Spider water into sudden, shivery columns of spray ;
then he wired, " ice out," and set back dragged
and silent for home and for sleep — ten hours out
of two hundred, maybe, was all he reckoned to the
good when he struck a pillow again.   Saturday
night he slept and Sunday all day and Sunday night.
Monday about noon Bucks sent up to ask, but Hailey
was asleep ; they asked back by the lad whether
they should wake him ; Bucks sent word, " No."

Tuesday morning the tall roadmaster came
down fresh as sunshine and all day he worked with
Bucks and the despatchers watching the line.   The
Spider raced like the Missouri, and the men at
the bridge sent in panic messages every night and
morning, but Hailey lit his pipe with their alarms.
" That bridge will go when the mountains go,"
was all he said.

Tuesday was his wedding date, old Denis told
Peeto; it was Hailey's wooden wedding, and when he
found everybody knew they were going to have a little spread over at the cottage, Hailey invited the boys
up for the evening.   Just a little celebration, Hailey
said, and everybody he spoke wrung his hand and
slapped his iron shoulders till Hailey echoed good
cheer through and through.   Callahan was going
over; Bucks had promised to look in, and Ed Peeto
and the boys had a little surprise for Hailey, had it
in the dark of the baggage-room in the Wickiup, a
big Morris chair.   No one would ever guess how
it landed at Medicine Bend, but it was easy.   Ed
Peeto had pulled it badly demoralized out of a
freight wreck at the Sugar Buttes and done it over
in company screws and varnish to surprise Hailey.
The anniversary made it just right, very hot stuff,
Ed Peeto said, and the company had undoubtedly
paid a claim voucher, for it — or would.

It was nine o'clock, night, and every star blink-
ing when Hailey looked in again at the office for
the track-walkers' reports and the Railway weather

bulletins.   Bucks, Callahan, and Peeto sat about
Duffy, who in his shirt-sleeves threw the stuff out
off the sounder as it trickled in dot and dash, dot
and dash over the wires.   The west wire was good
but east everything below Peace River was down.
We had to get the eastern reports around by Omaha
and the south — a good thousand miles of a loop —
but bad news travels even round a Robin Hood loop.

And Wild Hat came first from the west with a
stationary river and the Loup creek falling — clear
— good night.   And Ed Peeto struck the table
heavily and swore it was well in the west.   Then
from the east came Prairie Portage, all the way round,
with a northwest rain, a rising river, and anchor ice
pounding the piers badly, track in fair shape and —
and —

The wire went wrong.   As Duffy knit his eyes
and tugged and cussed a little the wind outside took
up the message and whirled a bucket of rain against
the windows.   But the wires would n't right and stuff
that no man could get tumbled in like a dictionary
upside down.   And Bucks and Callahan and Hailey

and Peeto smoked, silent, and listened to the deepening drum of the rain on the roof.

Then Duffy wrestled mightily yet once more, and the long way came word of trouble in the Omaha yards with the river at twenty-two feet and cutting; rising at Bismarck one foot an hour.

"Hell to pay on the Missouri, *of* course," growled the foreman, staring single-eyed at the inoffensive bulletin. "Well, she don't run our way; let her boil, damn her."

"Keep still," exclaimed Duffy, leaning heavily on the key. "Here's something — from — the Spider."

Only the hum of the rain and the nervous break of the sounder cut the smoke that curled from the pipes. Duffy snatched a pen and ran it across a clip, and Bucks leaning over read aloud from his shoulder:

"Omaha.

"J. F. Bucks.—Trainmen from Number Seventy-Five stalled west of Rapid City — track afloat in Simpson's cut — report Spider bridge out send —"

And the current broke.

Callahan's hand closed rigidly over his pipe; Peeto sat speechless; Bucks read again at the broken message, but Hailey sprang like a man wounded and snatched the clip from his superintendent's hand.

He stared at the running words till they burnt his eyes and then, with an oath, frightful as the thunder that broke down the mountains, he dashed the clip to the floor. His eyes snapped greenish with fury and he cursed Omaha, cursed its messages and everything that came out of it. Slow at first, but bitter, then fast and faster until all the sting that poisoned his heart in his unjust discharge poured from his lips. It flooded the room like a spilling stream and no man put a word against it for they knew he stood a wronged man. Out it came — all the rage — all the heart-burning — all the bitterness — and he dropped, bent, into a chair and covered his face with his hands: only the sounder clicking iron jargon and the thunder shaking the Wickiup like a reed filled the ears about him. They watched him slowly knot his fingers and loosen them, and saw his face rise dry and hard and old out of his hands.

" Get up an engine ! "

" Not — you 're not going down there to-night ? " stammered Bucks.

" Yes.   Now.   Right off.   Peeto !   Get out your crew ! "

The foreman jumped for the door ; Bucks hesitated barely an instant, then turning where he sat cut a telephone plug into the roundhouse ; Callahan saw him act and leaning forward spoke low to Duffy. The despatcher snatching the train sheet began instantly clearing track for a bridge special.

In twenty minutes twenty men were running twenty ways through the storm and a live engine boomed under the Wickiup windows.

" Phil, I want you to be careful ! "   It was Bucks standing by the roadmaster's side at the window as they looked out into the storm.   " It 's a bad night."   Hailey made no answer.   " A wicked night," muttered Bucks as the lightning shot the yards in a blaze and a crash rolled down the gorge. But wicked as it was he could not bring himself to countermand ; something forbade it.   Evans the conductor of the special ran in.

"Here's your orders!" exclaimed Duffy. Evans pulling down his storm cap nodded as he took the tissue. Hailey buttoned his leather jacket and turned to Bucks.

"Good-by."

"Mind your track," said Bucks, warningly to Evans as he took Hailey's hand. "What's your permit?"

"Forty miles an hour."

"Don't stretch it. Good-by, Phil," he added, speaking to Hailey. "I'll see you in the morning."

"In the morning," repeated Hailey. "Good-by. Nothing more in, Duffy?"

"Nothing more."

"Come on!" With the words he pushed the conductor through the door and was gone. The switch engine puffed up with the caboose. Ahead of it Ed Peeto had coupled in the pile driver. At the last minute Callahan asked to go, and as the bridge gang tumbled into the caboose, the assistant superintendent, Ed Peeto, and Hailey climbed into the engine. Denis Mullenix sat on the right and with

William Durden, fireman, they pulled out, five in the cab, for the Spider Water.

From Medicine Bend to the Spider Water is a ninety mile run ; down the gorge, through the foot-hills and into the Painted Desert that fills the jaw of the spur we intersect again west of Peace River. From the Peace to the Spider the crow flies twenty miles, but we take thirty for it ; there is hardly a tangent between.   Their orders set a speed limit, but from the beginning they crowded it.   Hailey, moody at first, began joking and laughing the minute they got away.   He sat behind Denis Mullenix on the right and poked at his ribs and taunted him with his heavy heels.   After a bit he got down and threw coal for Durden, mile after mile, and crowded the boiler till the safety screamed. When Durden took the shovel Hailey put his hand on the shoulder of Callahan, who was trying to hang to big Ed Peeto on the fireman's seat.

" Callahan," he yelled in his ear, " a man 's better off ——" And Callahan, though he could n't, in the pound and the roar, catch the words, nodded

and laughed because Hailey fiercely laughed.   Then
going around to the right the roadmaster covered
Denis Mullenix's fingers on the throttle latch and
the air with his big hands and good-naturedly coaxed
them loose, pushed the engineer back and got the
whip and the reins into his own keeping.   It was
what he wanted, for he smiled as he drew out the
bar a notch and settled himself for the run across
the flat country.   They were leaving the foothills,
and when the lightning opened the night they could
see behind through the blasting rain the great hulk-
ing pile driver nod and reel out into the Painted
Desert like a drunken man; for Hailey's schedule
was the wind and his limit the wide throttle.

The storm shook them with freshening fury and
drove the flanges into the south rail with a grinding
shriek, as they sped from the shelter of the hills.
The rain fell in a sheet, and the right of way ran
a river.   The wind, whipping the water off the
ballast, dashed it like hail against the cab glass; the
segment of desert caught in the yellow of the headlight rippled and danced and swam in the storm

water, and Hailey pulled again at the straining throttle
and latched it wider.   Callahan hung with a hand
to a brace and a hand to Peeto, and every little
while looked back at the caboose dancing a horn-
pipe over the joints; Mullenix, working the injector, stared astonished at Hailey; but Durden grimly
sprinkled new blood into the white furnace and eyed
his stack.

Notch after notch Hailey drew, heedless of lurch
and jump; heedless of bed or curve; heedless of
track or storm; and with every spur at her cylinders the engine shook like a frantic horse.   Men
and monster alike lost thought of care and drunk
a frenzy in the deafening whirl that Hailey opened
across the swimming plain.

The Peace River hills loomed into the headlight
like moving pictures; before they could think it, the
desert was behind.   Callahan, white-faced, climbed
down, and passed from hand to hand by Durden and
Mullenix got his hands on Hailey's shoulders and
his lips to his ear.

"For God's sake, Phil, let up!"

Hailey nodded and choked the steam a little. Threw a hatful of air on the shoes, but more as a test than a check : the fire was in his blood and he slewed into the hills with a speed unslackened. From the rocks it is a down grade all the way to the cañon, and the wind blew them and the track pulled them and a frenzied man sat at the throttle. Just where the line crosses Peace River the track bends sharply in through the Needles to take the bridge.

The curve is a ten degree. As they struck it, the headlight shot far out upon the river — and they in the cab knew they were dead men. Instead of lighting the box of the truss the lamp lit a black and snaky flood sweeping over the abutment with yellow foam. The Peace had licked up Agnew's thirty-foot piles and his bridge was not.

Whatever could be done — and Hailey knew all — meant death to the cab. Denis Mullenix never moved; no man that knew Hailey would think of trying to supplant him even with death under the ponies. He did what a man could do. There was no chance anyway for the cab : but the caboose held twenty of his faithful men.

He checked — and with a scream from the flanges the special, shaking in the clutches of the air-brake, swung the curve.

Again, the roadmaster checked heavily. The leads of the pile driver swaying high above gravity center careened for an instant wildly to the tangent, then the monster machine, parting from the tender, took the elevation like a hurdle and shot into the trees, dragging the caboose after it. But engine and tender and five in the cab plunged head on into the Peace.

Not a man in the caboose was killed; it was as if Hailey had tempered the blow to its crew. They scrambled out of the splinters and on their feet, men and ready to do. One voice from below came to them through the storm, and they answered its calling. It was Callahan; but Durden, Mullenix, Peeto, Hailey, never called again.

At daybreak wreckers of the West End, swarming from mountain and plain, were heading for the Peace, and the McCloud gang — up — crossed the Spider on Hailey's bridge — on the bridge the coward trainmen had reported out, quaking as they did in the storm at the Spider foaming over its approaches. But Hailey's bridge stood — stands to-day.

Yet three days the Spider raged, and knew then its master, while he, three whole days sat at the bottom of the Peace clutching the engine levers in the ruins of Agnew's mistake.

And when the divers got them up, Callahan and Bucks tore big Peeto's arms from his master's body and shut his staring eye and laid him at his master's side. And only the Spider ravening at Hailey's caissons raged. But Hailey slept.

Held for Orders

The Striker's Story

McTERZA

The Striker's Story

McTERZA

I WOULD not call her common. Not that I would be afraid to, though most of the boys were more or less afraid of Mrs. Mullenix, but simply that it would n't be right — not in my opinion.

She kept a short order house, let that be admitted at once, but her husband was long a West End engineer. Denis Mullenix went into the Peace with Hailey and Ed Peeto and Durden the night of the big June water on the West End. The company did n't treat her just right. I was a strong company man, although I went out with the boys. But I say, and I 've always said, the company did *not* treat Mrs. Mullenix just right.

A widow, and penniless, she bought the eating-house at McCloud with the few hundreds they gave her.

There were five young Mullenixes, and they were, every one, star children, from Sinkers, who was foxy, to Kate, who was not merely fine, she was royal. Twenty, and straight, and true, with a complexion like sunrise and hair like a sunset. Kate kept the cottage going, and Mrs. Mullenix ruled personally in the eating-house and in the short order annex. Any one that has tasted a steak grilled swell in Chicago or in Denver, and tasted one broiled plain by Mrs. Mullenix in McCloud, half a block from the depot, can easily understand why the boys behaved well. As for her coffee, believe it or not, we owe most of our world-famous West End runs, not so much to the Baldwin Locomotive Works, renowned as they are, nor to Mr. George Westinghouse, prince of inventors though we rank him — but to the coffee drawn by Mrs. Mary Mullenix; honor where honor is due.

Mrs. Mullenix's coffee for many years made the

boys hot: what now makes them hot is that she can't be persuaded to draw it for anybody except McTerza, and they claim that's the way he holds the Yellow Mail with the 808; but all the same McTerza is fast stuff, coffee or no coffee.

They were none of them boisterous men, those Reading engineers who took our jobs after the strike; but McTerza was an oyster, except that he could n't be swallowed.

McTerza did n't give up very much to anybody; not even to his own chums, Foley and Sinclair. The fact is he was diffident, owing, maybe, to a hesitation in his speech. It was funny, the bit of a halt, but not so odd as his disposition, which approached that of a grizzly. He had impudence and indifference and quiet — plenty of each.

There was one place up street that was, in special and particular, headquarters for the bad men in our crowd — for we had some — Gatling's billiard hall. Foley himself never had the nerve to tackle Gatling's. But one night, all alone and come from nobody knew where, the hall stuffed with striking

men who had tasted blood that very day — McTerza
walked into Gatling's.

It was like a yearling strolling into a cañon full
of wolves. They were so surprised at first they
could n't bite, but pretty soon they got McTerza
up against a mirror and began pasting pool balls at
him.

When Ed Banks arrived it was as bad as a rapid-
fire gun, and he carried McTerza out the side door
like a warm tapioca pudding. When the fellow got
round again, though, he was just as careless as ever.

It was pretty generally understood that in the
strike the short order house was with us. Mrs.
Mullenix had reason to feel bitter toward the company, and it became speedily known that Mrs.
Mullenix's was not a healthy place for the men
who took our engines ; their money was not wanted.
In fact, none of the new men ever tried to get
service there except McTerza. McTerza one
morning dropped into the short order house.

" Coffee," said he ; he always cut things short
because he was afraid he would get hung up between

stations in remarks. Mrs. Mullenix, sick, had to manage as she could. Kate was looking after things that day at the restaurant, and she was alone. She looked at McTerza chillingly. Kate had more than enough instinct to tell a Reading man from the Brotherhood type. She turned in silence, and she poured a cup of coffee, but from the night tank : it was the grossest indignity that could be perpetrated on a man in the short order management. She set it with little of civility and less of sugar before McTerza, and pushing her girdle down, coldly walked front, half perched on a stool, and looked listlessly out the window.

" Cool," ventured McTerza as he stirred a lump of sugar hopefully into his purchase. Kate made no comment on the observation ; the thing appeared self-evident.

" Could I have a little c-c-condensed milk ? " inquired McTerza presently. " This sc-sc-scream looks pretty rich," he added, stirring thoughtfully as he spoke at the pot of mustard, which was the only liquid in sight.

Kate Mullenix glared contemptuously at him, but she passed out a jug of cream — and it was cream. From the defiance on her face as she resumed her attitude she appeared to expect a protest about the cold coffee. None came. McTerza drank the stuff very slowly, blowing it carefully the while as if it was burning him up. It vexed Kate.

"How much?" asked McTerza humbly, as he swallowed the last drop before it froze to the spoon, and fished for a dime to square his account.

"Twenty-five cents." He started slightly but reached again into his pocket and without a word produced a quarter. Kate swept it into the drawer with the royal indifference of a circus faker and resumed her stool.

"C-c-could I get another c-c-cup?" asked McTerza patiently. It looked like a defiance; however she boldly poured a second cup of the cold coffee, and McTerza tackled it.

After an interval of silence he spoke again. "Do you sell tickets on c-coffee here?" She looked at him with a questioning insolence. "I mean, c-could a fellow buy a chance — or get into a raffle — on the h-h-h-hot tank?" asked McTerza, throwing a sad glance on the live coffee urn, which steamed cozily beside its silent companion.

"That tank is empty," snapped Kate Mullenix recklessly, for in spite of herself she was getting confused.

"If it is," suggested McTerza, peering gravely underneath at the jet of gas that blazed merrily, "you ought to draw your fire: you're liable to b-b-burn your c-c-crown-sheet."

"What's the matter?" demanded Kate angrily; "is your coffee cold?"

"Oh, no," he responded, shaking his head and waiting for the surprising disclaimer to sink in. "Not exactly cold. It's just dead."

"We don't serve Reading men here," retorted Kate defiantly.

"Oh, yes, you do," responded McTerza, brightening at once. "You serve them like t-t-tramps." Then after a pause: "Could I get a cigar?"

" Yes."

" How much is that kind ? "

" Fifty cents," snapped Kate, glancing into the street for some friendly striker to appear.

" I want a good one."

" That 's a good one."

" Fifty cents a b-b-box ? "

" Fifty cents apiece."

" Give me a small one, please."

He put down a dollar bill as he took the cigar. She threw a half back on the case. At that moment in walked two of our boys, Curtis Rucker and Ben Nicholson. McTerza had a great chance to walk out, but he did n't improve it. Rucker and Ben were Reds, both of them. Ben, in fact, was an old terror at best. Curtis Rucker was a blackish, quick young fellow, fine as silk in a cab, but a devil in a strike, and what was more, a great admirer of Kate Mullenix, and the minx knew it. As McTerza bit off the end of his cigar and reached for the gas-lighter he noticed that her face lighted wonderfully.

With a smile the newcomers called for coffee, and with a smile they got it. McTerza, smoking quietly at the cigar-case, watched the steaming liquid pour from the empty tank. It was a dispiriting revelation, but he only puffed leisurely on. When Kate glanced his way, as she presently did, disdainfully, McTerza raised his finger, and pointed to the change she had thrown at him.

" What is it, sir ? "

" Mistake."

The strikers pricked up their ears.

" There is n't any mistake, sir.   I told you the cigars were fifty cents each," replied Kate Mullenix. Rucker pushed back his coffee, and sliding off his stool walked forward.

" Change is n't right," persisted McTerza, looking at Kate Mullenix.

" Why not ? "

" You forgot to take out twenty-five cents more for that last cup of c-c-coffee," stammered the Reading man.   Kate took up the coin and handed a quarter back from the register.

" That 's right," put in Rucker promptly, " make the scabs p-p-pay for what they g-g-get. They 're sp-p-p-pending our money." The hesitating Reading man appeared for the first time aware of an enemy ; interested for the first time in the abuse that had been continually heaped on him since he came to town : it appeared at last to reach him. He returned Rucker's glare.

" You call me a scab, do you ? " he said at last and with the stutter all out. " I belong to a labor order that counts thousands to your hundreds. Your scabs came in and took our throttles on the Reading — why should n't we pull your latches out here ? Your strike is beat, my buck, and Reading men beat it. You had better look for a job on a threshing machine."

Rucker jumped for McTerza, and they mixed like clouds in a cyclone. For a minute it was a whirlwind, and nothing could be made of it ; but when they could be seen McTerza had the best man in our camp pinned under a table with his throat in one hand like the latch of a throttle.

Nicholson at the same moment raising an oak stool smashed it over McTerza's head. The fellow went flat as a dead man, but he must have pulled up quick, for when Neighbor, rushing in, whirled Nicholson into the street, the Reading man already had his feet, and a corner to work from. Reed, the trainmaster, was right behind the big master mechanic. Rucker was up, but saw he was outnumbered.

" Hurt, Mac ? " asked Reed, running toward the Reading man. The blow had certainly dazed him ; his eyes rolled seasick for a minute, then he stared straight ahead.

" Look out," he muttered, pointing over Reed's shoulder at Kate Mullenix, " she 's going to faint." The trainmaster turned, but Kate was over before her brother Sinkers could reach her as he ran in. Rucker moved towards the door. As he passed McTerza he sputtered villanously, but Neighbor's huge bulk was between the two men.

" Never mind," retorted McTerza ; " next time

I get you I'll ram a billiard c-c-c-cue down your throat."

It was the first intimation our fighting men had that the Reading fellow could do business, and the affair caused McTerza to be inspected with some interest from behind screens and cracker boxes as he sauntered up and down the street. When the boys asked him what he was going to do about his treatment in the short order house he seemed indifferent; but the indifference, as our boys were beginning to find out, covered live coals; for when he was pressed he threw the gauntlet at the whole lodge of us, by saying that before he got through he would close the short order house up. That threat made him a marked man. The Reading men were hated; McTerza was slated for the very worst of it. Everybody on both sides understood that — except McTerza himself. He never understood anything, for that matter, till it was on him, and he dropped back into his indifference and recklessness almost at once. He even tried the short order house again. That time Mrs. Mullenix

herself was in the saddle. There were things in
life which even McTerza did n't hanker after tack-
ling more than once, and one was a second interview
with Mrs. Mullenix. But the fellow must have
made an impression on even the redoubtable Mrs.
Mary, for she privately asked Neighbor, as one
might of an honorable adversary, for peace' sake
to keep that man away from her restaurant; so
McTerza was banned. He took his revenge by
sauntering in and out of Gatling's, until Gatling
himself went gray-headed with the fear that another
riot would be brought on his place.

Oddly enough, McTerza had one friend in the
Mullenix family. On the strike question, like
many other McCloud families, the house of Mullenix was divided against itself. All held for the
engineers except the youngest member, Sinkers.
Sinkers was telegraph messenger, and was strictly
a company man in spite of everything. He natu-
rally saw a great deal of the new men, but Sinkers
never took the slightest interest in McTerza till
he handled Rucker; after that Sinkers cultivated

him.   Sinkers would listen just as long as McTerza would stutter, and they became fast friends long before the yard riots.

The day the carload of detectives was imported the fight was on.   Scattering collisions breaking here and there into open fights showed the feeling, but it was n't till Little Russia went out that things looked rocky for the company property at McCloud. Little Russia had become a pretty big Russia at the time of the strike.   The Russians, planted at Benkleton you might say by Shockley, had spread up and down the line like tumbleweeds, and their first cousins, the Polacks, worked the company coal mines.   At McCloud they were as hard a crowd after dark as you would find on the steppes.   The Polacks, four hundred of them, struck while the engineers were out, and the fat went into the fire with a flash.

The night of the trouble took even us by surprise, and the company was wholly unprepared.   The engineers in the worst of the heat were accused of the rioting, but we had no more to do with it than homesteaders. Our boys are Americans, and we don't fight with torches and kerosene. We don't have to ; they 're not our weapons. The company imported the Polacks, let them settle their own accounts with them, said our fellows, and I called it right. Admitting that some of our Reds got out to mix in it, we could n't in sense be held for that.

It was Neighbor, the craftiest old fox on the staff of the division, who told the depot people in the afternoon that something was coming, and thinking back afterward of the bunches of the low-browed fellows dotting the bench and the bottoms in front of their dugouts, lowering at the guards who patrolled the railroad yards, it was strange no one else saw it. They had been out three weeks, and after no end of gabbling turned silent. Men that talk are not so dangerous ; it 's when they quit talking.

Neighbor was a man of a thousand to act on his apprehension. All the afternoon he had the switch engines shunting cars about the roundhouse ; the minute the arc lights went on the result could be

seen. The old man had long lines of furniture
vans, box cars, gondolas, and dead Pullmans strung
around the big house like parapets. Whatever anybody else thought, Neighbor was ready. Even old
John Boxer, his head blacksmith, who operated an
amateur battery for salutes and celebrations, had his
gun overhauled : the roundhouse was looking for
trouble.

It was barely eight o'clock that night when a
group of us on Main Street saw the depot lights go
out, and pretty soon telephone messages began
coming in to Gatling's from the company plant up
the river for the sheriff; the Polacks were wrecking
the dynamos. The arc lights covering the yards
were on a different circuit, but it did n't take the
whiskered fellows long to find that out. Half an
hour later the city plant was attacked ; no one was
looking for trouble there, and the great system of
arcs lighting the yard for miles died like fireflies.
We knew then, everybody knew, that the Polacks
meant business.

Not a man was in sight when the blaze sputtered

blue, red, and black out; but in five minutes a dozen
torches were moving up on the in-freight house like
coyotes. We could hear the crash of the big oak
doors clear down on Main Street. There, again,
the company was weak; they had n't a picket out
at either of the freight houses. There was n't so
much as a sneeze till they beat the doors in; then
there was a cry; the women were taking a hand,
and it was a loot with a big L. The plunder maddened them like brandy. Neighbor, who feared
not the Polacks nor the devil, made a sortie with a
dozen men from his stockade, for that was what the
roundhouse defenses looked like, to try to save the
building. It was n't in men to do it. The gutting
was done and the kerosene burning yellow before
he was half-way across, and the mob, running then
in a wavering black line from the flames that licked
the high windows, were making for the storehouse.
The fellows were certainly up to everything good,
for in plundering the freight house first they gave
their women the chance to lay in supplies for months.
Neighbor saw in a minute there was nothing left

for him to protect at the east end, and before he could cut off the constantly lengthening line of rioters, they were between him and the long storehouse.   It must have made the old man weep blood, and it was there that the first shooting occurred.

A squad of the detectives reënforcing Neighbor's little following, ran in on the flank of the rioters as the master mechanic caught up with their rear. They wheeled, on his command to disperse, and met it with a cloud of stones and coupling pins. The detectives opened with their Winchesters, and a yell went up that took me back to the Haymarket. Their answer was the torch to the storehouse and a charge on the imported guards that shook their front like a whirlwind.   The detectives ran for Neighbor's breastworks, with the miners hot behind, and a hail of deadly missiles on their backs.   One went down at the turn-table, and it did n't look as if his life was worth a piece of waste. But the fellow, raising on one arm, began picking off the Polacks closest with a revolver.   They scattered like turkeys, and he staggered across the table before they could damage him any worse. Half a dozen of us stood in the cupola of the fire-engine house, with the thing laid below like a panorama.

Far as the blazing freight house lit the yards, we could see the rioters swarming in from the bottoms. The railroad officials gathered up stairs in the passenger depot waited helpless for the moment when the fury of the mob should turn on the unprotected building. The entire records of the division, the despatchers' offices, the headquarters of the whole West End were under that roof, with nothing to stand between it and the torches.

Awkwardly as the rioters had maneuvered, they seemed then to be getting into better shape for mischief. They were quicker at expedients, and two intensely active leaders rose out of the crowds. Following the shouts of the pair, which we could just hear, a great body of the strikers dashed up the yard.

" By the Gods ! " cried Andy Cameron at my elbow, " they 're going for the oil-house ! "

Before the words were out we could hear the

dull stroke of the picks sinking into the cleated
doors. Buckets were passed in and out from the
house tanks. Jacketed cans of turpentine and varnish were hustled down the line to men drunk with
riot; in a moment twenty cars were ablaze. To
top the frenzy they fired the oil-house itself. Destruction crazed the entire population of the
bottoms. The burning cars threw the front of the
big brick depot up into the sky. As the reflec-
tion struck back from the plate-glass windows, the
mob split into two great waves, and one headed
for the passenger depot. They crossed the coal
spurs brandishing torches and sledges and bars.
We could see them plain as block signals. Every
implement that ever figured in a yard showed in
their line, but their leader, a youngish fellow, swung
a long, tapering stake. As the foremost Polack
climbed up on the last string of flats that separated
them from the depot, the storage tanks in the oil-
house took fire. The roof jumped from the wall-
plates like one vast trap-door, and the liquid yellow
spurted flaming a hundred feet up into the black.

A splitting yell greeted the burst, and the Polacks, with added fury, raced towards the long depot.   I made out then the man with the club.   It was Rucker.

The staff of the superintendent, and the force of despatchers, a handful of men all told, gathered at the upper windows and opened fire with revolvers. It was just enough to infuriate the rioters.   And it appeared certain that the house would be burned under the defenders' feet, for the broad platform was bare from end to end.   Not a ghost of a bar-ricade, not a truck, not a shutter stood between the depot and the torch, and nobody thought of a man until Cameron with the quicker eyes cried :

" For God's sake !   There's McTerza ! "

Such as pay-day there he was, walking down the platform towards the depot, and humping alongside — Sinkers.

I guess everybody in both camps swore.   Like a man in his sleep he was walking right in the teeth of the Polacks.   If we had tried ourselves to pit him it could n't have been done cleaner.   His friends,

for McTerza had them, must have shivered — but
that was just McTerza; to be where he should n't,
when he should n't. Even had there not been more
pressing matters, nobody could have figured out
where the fellow had come from with his convoy,
or where he was going. He was there; that was
all — he was there.

The despatchers yelled at him from above. The
cry echoed back short from a hundred Polack throats,
and they sent a splitter; it was plain they were mad
for blood. Even that cry did n't greatly faze the
fellow, but in the clatter of it all he caught another
cry — a cry sent straight to McTerza's ear, and
he turned at the voice and the word like a man
stung. Rucker, leaping ahead and brandishing the
truck-stake at the hated stutterer, yelled, "The
scab!"

The Reading engineer halted like a baited bear.

Rucker's cry was enough — in that time and at
that place it was enough. McTerza froze to the
platform. There was more — and we knew it, all
of us — more between those two men than scab

and brotherhood, strike and riot, flood or fire : there was a woman. We knew it so well there was hardly a flutter anywhere, I take it, when men saw McTerza stooping, grasp Sinkers, shove him towards the depot, slip like a snake out of his pea-jacket, and turn to front the whole blooming mob. There was n't any fluttering, I take it — and not very much breathing ; only the scab, never a tremendous big man, swelled bigger in the eyes then straining his way than any man in McCloud has ever swelled before or since.

Mobs are queer. A minute before it was the depot, now it was the scab — kill him.

The scab stood. Rucker stumbled across a rail in his fury, and went sprawling, but the scab stood. The line wavered like tumbleweeds. They did n't understand a man fronting forty. Then Ben Nicholson — I recognized his whiskers — began blazing at him with a pistol. Yet the scab stood and halted the Polack line. They hesitated, they stopped to yell; but the scab stood.

"Stone him!" shouted Ben Nicholson. McTerza

backed warily across the platform. The Polacks wavered; the instinct of danger unsettled them. Mobs are queer. A single man will head them quicker than a hundred guns. There is nothing so dangerous as one man.

McTerza saw the inevitable, the steady circling that must get him at last, and as the missiles flew at him from a score of miners he crouched with the rage of a cornered rat, one eye always on Rucker.

" Come in, you coyote ! " yelled McTerza tauntingly. " Come in ! " he cried, catching up a coupling pin that struck him and hurling it wickedly at his nearest assailant. Rucker, swinging his club, ran straight at his enemy.

" Kill the scab ! " he cried and a dozen bristling savages, taking his lead, closed on the Reading man like a fan. From the windows above, the railroad men popped with their pistols; they might as well have thrown fire-crackers. McTerza, with a cattish spring, leaped through a rain of brickbats for Rucker.

Old Man Nicholson.

The club in the striker's hands came around with sweep enough to drop a steer. Quick as a sounder key McTerza's head bobbed, and he went in and under on Rucker's jaw with his left hand. The man's head twisted with the terrific impact like a Chinese doll's. Down he went, McTerza, hungry, at his throat; and on top of McTerza the Polacks, with knives and hatchets and with Cossack barks, and they closed over him like water over a stone.

Nobody ever looked to see him pull out, yet he wormed his way through them corkscrew fashion, while they hacked at one another, and sprang out behind his assailants with Rucker's club. In his hands it cut through guards and arms and knives like toothpicks. Rucker was smothering under toppling Polacks. But others ran in like rats. They fought McTerza from side to side of the platform. They charged him and flanked him — once they surrounded him — but his stanchion swung every way at once. Swarm as they would, they could not get a knife or a pick into him, and it looked as

if he would clear the whole platform, when his
dancing eye caught a rioter at the baggage room
door mercilessly clubbing poor little Sinkers.   The
boy lay in a pitiful heap no better than a dying
mouse.   McTerza, cutting his way through the
circle about him, made a swath straight for the kid,
and before the brute over him could run he brought
the truck-stake with a full-arm sweep flat across
his back.   The man's spine doubled like a jack-
knife, and he sunk wriggling.   McTerza made but
the one pass at him ; he never got up again.   Catching Sinkers on his free arm, the Reading man ran
along the depot front, pulling him at his side and
pounding at the doors.   But every door was barred,
and none dared open.   He was clean outside the
breastworks, and as he trotted warily along, dragging
the insensible boy, they cursed and chased and
struck him like a hunted dog.

At the upper end of the depot stands a huge ice-
box.   McTerza, dodging in the hail that followed
him, wheeling to strike with a single arm when
the savages closed too thick, reached the recess,

and throwing Sinkers in behind, turned at bay on his enemies.

With his clothes torn nearly off, his shirt streaming ribbons from his arms, daubed with dirt and blood, the scab held the recess like a giant, and beat down the Polacks till the platform looked a slaughter pen. While his club still swung, old John Boxer's cannon boomed across the yard. Neighbor had run it out between his parallels, and turned it on the depot mob. It was the noise more than the execution that dismayed them. McTerza's fight had shaken the leaders, and as the blacksmiths dragged their gun up again, shotted with nothing more than an Indian yell, McTerza's assailants gave way. In that instant he disappeared through the narrow passage at his back, and under the shadow behind the depot made his way along the big building and up Main Street to the short order house. Almost unobserved he got to the side door, when Rucker's crowd, with Rucker again on his feet, spied him dragging Sinkers inside. They made a yell and a dash, but McTerza got the boy in and the door barred before they could reach it. They ran to the front, baffled. The house was dark and the curtains drawn. Their clamor brought Mrs. Mullenix, half dead with fright, to the door. She recognized Nicholson and Rucker, and appealed to them.

" Pray God, do you want to mob *me*, Ben Nicholson ? " she sobbed, putting her head out fearfully.

" We want the scab that sneaked into the side door, Mrs. Mary ! " roared Ben Nicholson. " Fire him out here."

" Sure there 's no one here you want."

" We know all about that," cried Rucker breaking in. " We want the scab." He pushed her back and crowded into the door after her.

The room was dark, but the fright was too great for Mrs. Mullenix, and she cried to McTerza to leave her house for the love of God. Some one tore down the curtains ; the glow of the burning yards lit the room, and out of the gloom, behind the lunch counter, almost at her elbow — a desperate sight, they told me — panting, blood-stained, and torn, rose McTerza. His fingers closed over the grip of the bread-knife on the shelf beside him.

"Who wants me?" he cried, leaning over his breastwork.

"Leave my house! For the love of God, leave it!" screamed Mrs. Mullenix, wringing her hands. The scab, knife in hand, leaped across the counter. Nicholson and Rucker bumped into each other at the suddenness of it, but before McTerza could spring again there was a cry behind.

"He sha'n't leave this house!" And Kate Mullenix, her face ablaze, strode forward. "He sha'n't leave this house!" she cried again, turning on her mother. "Leave this house, after he's just pulled your boy from under their cowardly clubs! Leave it for who? He sha'n't go out. Burn it over our heads!" she cried passionately, wheeling on the rioters. "When he goes we'll go with him. It's you that want him, Curtis Rucker, is it? Come, get him, you coward! There he stands. Take him!"

Her voice rang like a fire-bell. Rucker, burnt
by her words, would have thrown himself on
McTerza, but Nicholson held him back.   There
never would have been but one issue if they had
met then.

"Come away!" called the older man hoarsely.
"It's not women we're after.   She's an engineer's
wife, Curt; this is her shanty.   Come away, I say,"
and saying, he pushed Rucker and their coyote
following out of the door ahead of him.   Mrs.
Mullenix and Kate sprang forward to lock the
door.   As they ran back, McTerza, spent with
blood, dropped between them.   So far as I can
learn that is where the courtship began, right then
and there — and as McTerza says, all along of
Sinkers, for Sinkers was always Kate's favorite
brother, as he is now McTerza's.

Sinkers had a time pulling through after the
clubbing.   Polacks hit hard.   There was no end
of trouble before he came out of it, but sinkers are
tough, and he pulled through, only to think more
of McTerza than of the whole executive staff.

At least that is the beginning of the courtship as I got it. There was never any more trouble about serving the new men at the short order house that I ever heard ; and after the rest of us got back to work we ate there side by side with them. McTerza got his coffee out of the hot tank, too, though he always insisted on paying twenty-five cents a cup for it, even after he married Kate and had a kind of an interest in the business.

It was not until then that he made good his early threat. Sinkers being promoted for the toughness of his skull, thought he could hold up one end of the family himself, and McTerza expressed confidence in his ability to take care of the other ; so, finally, and through his persuasions, the short order house was closed forever. Its coffee to-day is like the McCloud riots, only a stirring memory.

As for McTerza, it is queer, yet he never stuttered after that night, not even at the marriage service ; he claims the impediment was scared clean out of him. But that night made the reputation of McTerza a classic among the good men of McCloud. McCloud has, in truth, many good men, though the head of the push is generally conceded to be the husband of royal Kate Mullenix — Johnnie McTerza.

Held for Orders

The Despatcher's Story

THE LAST ORDER

The Despatcher's Story

✻

THE LAST ORDER

IN order to meet objection on the score of the impossible, and to anticipate inquiry as to whether "The Despatcher's Story" is true, it may be well to state frankly at the outset that this tale, in its inexplicable psychological features, is a transcript from the queer things in the railroad life. It is based on an extraordinary happening that fell within the experience of the president of a large Western railway system. Whether the story, suggestive from any point of view of mystery, can be regarded as a demonstration of the efficacy of prayer may be a disputable question. In passing, however, it is only fair to say that the circumstance on which the tale is based was so regarded by the despatcher himself, and by those familiar with the circumstance.

A HUNDRED times if once the thing had been, on appeals for betterment, before the board of directors. It was the one piece of track on the Mountain Division that trainmen shook their heads over — the Peace River stretch. To run any sort of a line through that cañon would take the breath of an engineer. Give him all the money he could ask and it would stagger Wetmore himself. Brodie in his day said there was nothing worse in the Andes, and Brodie, before he drifted into the Rockies, had seen, first and last, pretty much all of the Chilian work.

But our men had the job to do with one half the money they needed. The lines to run, the grades to figure, the culverts to put in, the fills to make, the blasting to do, the tunnel to bore, the bridge to build — in a limit; that was the curse of it — the

limit. And they did the best they could. But
I will be candid : if a section and elevation of
Rosamond's bower and a section and elevation of
our Peace River work were put up to stand for a
prize at a civil engineers' cake-walk the decision
would go, and quick, to the Peace River track.
There are only eight miles of it ; but our men
would back it against any eighty on earth for whipping curves, tough grades, villainous approaches,
and railroad tangle generally.

The directors always have promised to improve
it ; and they are promising yet. Thanks to what
Hailey taught them, there's a good bridge there
now — pneumatic caissons sunk to the bed. It's
the more pity they have n't eliminated the dread
main line curves that approach it, through a valley
which I brief as a cañon and the Mauvaises Terres
rolled into one single proposition.

Yet, we do lots of business along that stretch.
Our engineers thread the cuts and are glad to get
safely through them. Our roadmasters keep up the
elevations, hoping some night the blooming right

of way will tumble into perdition. Our despatchers, studying under shaded lamps, think of it with their teeth clinched and hope there never will be any trouble on that stretch. Trouble is our portion and trouble we must get; but not there. Let it come; but let it come anywhere except on the Peace.

It was in the golden days of the battered old Wickiup that the story opens; when Blackburn sat in the night chair. The days when the Old Guard were still there; before Death and Fame and Circumstance had stolen our first commanders and left only us little fellows, forgotten by every better fate, to tell their greater stories.

Hailey had the bridges then, and Wetmore the locating, and Neighbor the roundhouses, and Bucks the superintendency, and Callahan, so *he* claimed, the work, and Blackburn had the night trick.

I

WHEN Blackburn came from the plains he brought a record clean as the book of life.   Four years on a station key; then eight years at Omaha despatching, with never a blunder or a break to the eight years.   But it was at Omaha that Blackburn lost the wife whose face he carried in his watch.   I never heard the story, only some rumor of how young she was and how pretty, and how he buried her and the wee baby together.   It was all Blackburn brought to the West End mountains, his record and the little face in the watch.   They said he had no kith or kin on earth, besides the wife and the baby back on the bluffs of the Missouri; and so he came on the night trick to us.

I was just a boy around the Wickiup then, but I remember the crowd; who could forget them? They were jolly good fellows; sometimes there were very high jinks.   I don't mean anybody drunk

or that sort; but good tobacco to smoke and good
songs to sing and good stories to tell — and Lord !
how they could tell them. And when the pins
slipped, as they would, and things went wrong, as
they will, there were clear heads and pretty wits
and stout hearts to put things right.

Blackburn, as much as I can remember, always
enjoyed it ; but in a different way. He had such
times a manner like nobody else's — a silent, beam-
ing manner. When Bucks would roll a great white
Pan-Handle yarn over his fresh linen shirt-front and
down his cool clean white arms, one of them always
bared to the elbow — sanding his points with the
ash of a San Francisco cigar — and Neighbor would
begin to heave from the middle up like a hippopota-
mus, and Callahan would laugh his whiskers full
of dew, and Hailey would yell with delight, and the
slaves in the next room would double up on the
dead at the story, Blackburn would sit with his
laugh all in a smile, but never a noise or a word.
He enjoyed it all ; not a doubt of that ; only it was
all tempered, I reckon, by something that had gone

before.   At least, that's the way it now strikes me,
and I watched those big fellows pretty close — the
fellows who were to turn, while I was growing up
among them, into managers and presidents and magnates; and some of them from every day catch-as-
catch-can men with the common alkali flecking
their boots into dead men for whom marble never
rose white enough or high enough.

Blackburn was four years at the Wickiup on the
night trick; it would n't have seemed natural to
see him there in daylight.   It needed the yellow
gloom of the old kerosene lamp in the room; the
specked, knotted, warped, smoky pine ceiling losing itself in black and cobwebbed corners; the
smoldering murk of the soft-coal fire brooding in
the shabby old salamander, and, outside in the darkness, the wind screwing down the gorge and rattling
the shrunken casements, to raise Blackburn in the
despatcher's chair.   Blackburn and the lamp and
the stove and the ceiling and the gloom — in a word,
Blackburn and the night trick — they went together.

Before the Short line was opened the Number

One and Number Five trains caught practically all
the coast passenger business. They were immensely
heavy trains; month after month we sent out two
and three sections of them each way, and they always
ran into our division on the night trick.   Blackburn
handled all that main line business with a mileage
of eight hundred and five, besides the mountain
branches, say four hundred more; and the passenger connections came off them, mostly at night, for
One and Five.

Now, three men wrestle with Blackburn's mileage; but that was before they found out that despatchers, although something tougher than steel, do
wear out.   Moreover, we were then a good way
from civilization and extra men.   If a despatcher
took sick there was no handy way of filling in; it
was just double up and do the best you could.

One lad in the office those days everybody
loved: Fred Norman.   He was off the Burlington.   A kid of a fellow who looked more like
a choir boy than a train despatcher.   But he was
all lightning — a laughing, restless, artless boy,

open as a book and quick as a current.   There was
a better reason still, though, why they loved Fred :
the boy had consumption ; that's why he was out
in the mountains, and his mother in Detroit used
to write Bucks asking about him, and she used to
send us all things in Fred's box.   His flesh was as
white and as pink as mountain snow, and he had
brown eyes; he was a good boy, and I called him
handsome.   I reckon they all did.   Fred brought
out a tennis set with him, the first we ever saw in
Medicine Bend, and before he had been playing an
hour he had Neighbor, big as a grizzly, and Callahan, with a pipe in one hand and a tennis guide in
the other, chasing all over the yard after balls; and
Hailey trying to figure forty love, while Fred taught
Bucks the Lawford drive.   I don't say what he was
to me ; only that he taught me all I ever knew or
ever will know about handling trains ; and, though
I was carrying messages then, and he was signing
orders, we were really like kids together.

Fred for a long time had the early trick.   He
came on at four in the morning and caught most

of the through freights that got away from the River behind the passenger trains.   There was no use trying to move them in the night trick.   Between the stock trains eastbound and the both-way passenger trains, if a westbound freight got caught in the mountains at night the engine might as well be standing in the house saving fuel — there was n't time to get from one siding to another.   So Fred Norman took the freights as they came and he handled them like a ringmaster.   When Fred's whip cracked, by Joe! a train had to dance right along, grade or no grade. Fred gave them the rights and they had the rest to do — or business to do with the superintendent or with Doubleday, Neighbor's assistant in the motive power.

There was only one tendency in Fred Norman's despatching that anybody could criticise: he never seemed, after handling trains on the plains, to appreciate what our mountain grades really meant, and when they pushed him he sent his trains out pretty close together.   It never bothered him to handle a heavy traffic; he would get the business through the

mountains just as fast as they could put it at the
Division; but occasionally there were some hair-
curling experiences among the freights on Norman's
trick trying to keep off each other's coat-tails. One
night in July there was a great press moving eight
or nine trains of Montana grassers over the main
line on some kind of a time contract — we were
giving stockmen the earth then. Everybody was
prodding the Mountain Division, and part of the
stuff came in late on Blackburn and part of it early
on Fred, who was almost coughing his head off about
that time, getting up at 3.30 every morning. Fred
at four o'clock took the steers and sent them train
after train through the Rat River country like bullets out of a Maxim gun. It was hot work, and
before he had sat in an hour there was a stumble.
The engineer of a big ten-wheeler pulling twenty-
five cars of steers had been pushing hard and, at
the entrance of the cañon, set his air so quick he
sprung one of the driver shoes and the main rod hit
it. The great steel bar doubled up like a man with
a cramp. It was showing daylight; they made a

stop, and, quick as men could do it, flagged both
ways.   But the last section was crowding into the
cañon right behind ; they were too close together,
that was all there was to it.   The hind section split
into the standing train like a butcher knife into a
sandwich.   It made a mean wreck — and, worse,
it made a lot of hard feeling at the Wickiup.

When the investigation came it was pretty near
up to Fred Norman right from the start, and he
knew it.   But Blackburn, who shielded him when
he could, just as all the despatchers did, because he
was a boy — and a sick one among men — tried to
take part of the blame himself.   He could afford it,
Blackburn ; his shoulders were broad and he had n't
so much as a fly-speck on his book.   Bucks looked
pretty grave when the evidence was all in, and around
the second floor they guessed that meant something
for Norman.   Fred himself could n't sleep over it,
and to complicate things the engineer of the stalled
train, who hated Doubleday, hinted quietly that the
trouble came in the first place from Doubleday's
new-fangled idea of putting the driver shoes behind

instead of in front of the wheels. Then the fat
was in the fire. Fred got hold of it, and, boy-like
— sore over his own share in the trouble and exas-
perated by something Doubleday was reported to
have said about *him* over at the house — lighted into
Doubleday about the engine failure.

Doubleday was right in his device, as time has
proved; but it was unheard of then and moreover, the assistant master mechanic sensitive to
criticism at any time, was a fearful man to run
against. Sunday morning he and Norman met in
the trainmaster's office. They went at each other
like sparks, and when Doubleday, who had a hard
mouth, began cursing Fred, the poor little despatcher, rankling with the trouble, anyway half
sick, went all to pieces and flew at the big fellow
like a sparrowhawk. He threw a wicked left into
the master mechanic before Doubleday could lift a
guard. But Walter Doubleday, angry as he was,
could n't strike Fred. He caught up both the
boy's hands and pushed him, struggling madly,
back against the wall to slap his face, when a

froth of blood stained Fred's lips and he fell fainting; just at that minute Blackburn stepped into the room.

It wasn't the kind of a time — they weren't the kind of men — to ask or volunteer explanations. Blackburn was on Doubleday in a wink, and before Walter could right himself the night despatcher had thrown him headlong across the room. As the operators rushed in, Blackburn and the tall master mechanic sprang at each other in a silent fury. No man dare say where it might have ended had not Fred Norman staggered between them with his hands up — but the blood was gushing from his mouth.

It was pretty serious business. They caught him as he fell, and the boy lay on Blackburn's arm limp as a dead wire: nobody thought after they saw that hemorrhage that he would ever live to have another. I was scared sick, and I never saw a man so cut up as Doubleday. Blackburn was cool in a second, for he saw quicker than others and he knew there was danger of the little de-

spatcher's dying right there in his tracks.   Blackburn stood over him, as much at home facing death
as he was in a fight or in a despatcher's chair.
He appeared to know just how to handle the boy
to check the gush, and to know just where the
salt was and how to feed it, and he had Doubleday telephoning for Dr. Carhart and me running
to a saloon after chopped ice in a jiffy.   When
anybody was knocked out, Blackburn was as regular a nurse as ever you saw; even switchmen, when
they got pinched, kind of looked to Blackburn.

That day the minute he got Fred into Carhart's
hands there was Fred's trick to take care of, and
nobody, of course, but Blackburn to do it.   He
sat in and picked up the threads and held them till
noon; then Maxwell relieved him.   Doubleday
was waiting outside when Blackburn left the
chair.   I saw him put out his hand to the night
despatcher.   They spoke a minute, and went out
and up Third Street toward Fred Norman's room.
It was a gloomy day around the depot.   Everybody was talking about the trouble, and the way it

had begun and the way it had ended. They talked in undertones, little groups in corners and in rooms with the doors shut. There was n't much of that in our day there, and it was depressing. I went home early to bed, for I was on nights. But the wind sung so, even in the afternoon, that I could n't quiet down to sleep.

II

WE were handling trains then on the old single-order system. I mention this because in no other way could this particular thing have happened; but there 's no especial point in that, since other particular things do happen all the time, single order, double order, or no order system.

The wind had dropped, and there was just a drizzle of rain falling through the mountains when I got down to the depot at seven o'clock that Sunday evening. I don't know how much sleep Blackburn had had during the day, but he had been at Fred Norman's bed most of the afternoon with Doubleday and Carhart, so he could n't have had much.   About half-past seven Maxwell sent me over there with a note and his storm-coat for him and the three men were in the room then. Boy-like, I hung around until it was time for Blackburn to take his trick, and then he and Doubleday and I walked over to the Wickiup together.

At sundown everything was shipshape.   There had n't been an engine failure in the district for twenty-four hours and every hand-car was running smoothly.   Moreover, there were no extra sections marked up and only one Special on the Division card — a theatrical train eastbound with Henry Irving and company from 'Frisco to Chicago.   The Irving Special was heavy, as it always is; that night there were five baggage cars, a coach and two sleepers.   I am particular to lay all this out just as the night opened when Blackburn took his train sheet, because sometimes these things happen under extraordinary pressure on the line and sometimes they don't; sometimes they happen under pressure on the despatcher himself. It was all fixed, too, for Blackburn to handle not only his own trick but the first two hours of Fred's trick, which would carry till six o'clock in the morning. At six Maxwell was to double into a four-hour dog-watch, and Callahan was to sit in till noon.

There was nothing to hold the big fellows around the depot that night, and they began straggling home through the rain about nine o'clock. Before ten, Bucks and Callahan had left the office; by eleven, Neighbor had got away from the roundhouse; Doubleday had gone back to sit with Fred Norman.

The lights in the yard were low and the drizzle had eased into a mist; it was a nasty night, and yet one never promised better for quiet. Before midnight the switchmen were snug in the yard shanties; in the Wickiup there were the night ticket agent downstairs and the night baggageman. Upstairs every door was locked and every room

was dark, except the despatcher's office.   In that,
Blackburn sat at his key; nearby, but closer to the
stove, sat the night caller for the train crews, trying to starch his hair with a ten-cent novel.

The westbound Overland passenger, Number
One, was due to leave Ames at 12.40 A. M.,
and ordinarily would have met a Special like the
Irving at Rosebud, which is a good bit west of
the river.   But Number One's engine had been
steaming badly all the way from McCloud, and
on her schedule, which was crazy fast all night,
she did not make Ames till some fifty minutes
late.   While there were no special orders, it
was understood we were to help the Irving train
as much as possible anyway.   Bucks had made
the acquaintance of the great man and his fellows
on the westbound run, and as they had paid us
the particular compliment of a return trip, we
were minded to give them the best of it — even
against Number One, which was always rather
sacred on the sheet.   This, I say, was pretty generally understood ; for when it was all over there

was no criticism whatever on Blackburn's intention of making a meeting-point for the two trains, as they then stood, at O'Fallon's siding.

Between Ames and Rosebud, twenty miles apart, there are two sidings — O'Fallon's, west of the river, and Salt Rocks, east. There was no operator at either place. The train that leaves Ames westbound is in the open for twenty miles with only schedule rights or a despatcher's tissue between her and the worst of it. At one o'clock that morning Blackburn wired an order to Ames for Number One to hold at O'Fallon's for Special 202. A minute later he sent an order for Special 202 to run to O'Fallon's regardless of Number One. At least, he thought he sent such an order; but he did n't — he made a mistake.

When he had fixed the meeting-point, Blackburn rose from his chair and sat down by the stove. I lazily watched him, till, falling into a doze as I eyed him drowsily, he began to loom up in his chair and to curl and twist toward the roof like a signal column; then the front legs of his chair struck the floor, and with a start I woke, just as he stepped hurriedly back to his table and picked up the order book.

The first suspicion I had that anything was wrong was an exclamation from Blackburn as he stared at the book. Putting it down almost at once and holding the page open with his left hand, he plugged Callahan's house wire and began drumming his call. Callahan's "Aye, aye," came back inside of a minute, and Blackburn tapped right at him: "Come down." And I began to wonder what *was* up.

There was an interval; then Callahan asked, "What's the matter?"

I got up and walked over to the water-tank for a drink. Blackburn again pressed the key, and repeated to Callahan precisely the words he had used before: "Come down."

His face was drawn into the very shape of fear and his eyes, bent hard on me, were looking through me and through the shivering window — I know it now — and through the storming night, horror-set, into the cañon of the Peace River.

The sounder broke and he turned back, listened
a moment; but it was stray stuff about time
freight. He pushed the chair from behind him,
still like a man listening — listening; then with
an effort, plain even to me, he walked across the
office, pushed open the door of Callahan's private
room, and stood with his hand on the knob, looking back at the lamp.   It was as if he still seemed
to listen, for he stood undecided a moment; then
he stepped into the dark room and closed the
door behind him, leaving me alone and dumb with
fear.

The mystery lay, I knew, in the order book.
Curiosity gradually got the better of my fright,
and I walked from the cooler over to the counter
to get courage, and shoved the train register
around noisily.   I crossed to the despatchers' table
and made a pretence of arranging the pads and
blanks.   The train order book was lying open
where he had left it under the lamp.   With my
eyes bulging, I read the last two orders copied
in it:

C. and E.   No. One, Ames.

    No. One, Eng. 871, will hold at O'Fallon's
      for Special 202.

C. and E. Special 202, Rosebud.

    Special 202, Eng. 636, will run to Salt Rocks
regardless of No. One.

SALT ROCKS! I glared at the words and
the letters of the words.

I re-read the first order and read again the second. O'Fallon's for Number One. That was
right. O'Fallon's it should be for the Special 202,
of course, to meet her. But it was n't: it was
the first station east of O'Fallon's he had ordered
the Special to run to. It was a lap order. My
scalp began to creep. A lap order for the Irving
Special and the Number One passenger, and it
doomed them to meet head on somewhere between
O'Fallon's and the Salt Rocks, in the Peace River
cañon.

My mouth went sticking dry. The sleet outside had deepened into a hail that beat the west
glass sharper and the window shook again in the

wind. I asked myself, afraid to look around, what Blackburn could be doing in Callahan's room. The horror of the wreck impending through his mistake began to grow on me; I know what I suffered; I ask myself now what he suffered, inside, alone, in the dark.

Oh, you who lie down upon the rail at night to sleep, in a despatcher's hand, think you, ever, in your darkened berths of the cruel responsibility on the man who in the watches of the night holds you in his keeping?

Others may blunder; others may forget; others may fall and stand again: not the despatcher; a single mistake damns him. When he falls he falls forever.

Young as I was, I realized that night the meaning of the career to which my little ambition urged me. The soldier, the officer, the general, the statesman, the president, may make mistakes, do make mistakes, that cost a life or cost ten thousand lives. They redeem them and live honored. It is the obscure despatcher under

the lamp who for a single lapse pays the penalty
of eternal disgrace. I felt something of it even
then, and from my boy's heart, in the face of the
error, in the face of the slaughter, I pitied Blackburn.

Callahan's room door opened again and Blackburn came out of the dark. I had left the table
and was standing in front of the stove. He looked
at me almost eagerly ; the expression of his face
had completely changed. I never in my life saw
such a change in so few minutes on any man's
face, and, like all the rest, it alarmed me. It was
not for me to speak if I had been able, and he
did not. He walked straight over to the table,
closed the order book, plugged Callahan's house
wire again, and began calling him. The assistant
superintendent answered, and Blackburn sent him
just these words :

"You need not come down."

I heard Callahan reply with a question : "What
is the matter ? "

Blackburn stood calmly over the key, but he

made no answer. Instead, he repeated only the words, "You need not come down."

Callahan, easily excitable always, was wrought up. "Blackburn," he asked over the wire, impatiently, "What in God's name is the matter?" But Blackburn only pulled the plug and cut him out, and sunk into the chair like a man wearied.

"Mr. Blackburn," I said, my heart thumping like an injector, "Mr. Blackburn?" He glanced vacantly around; seemed for the first time to see me. "Is there anything," I faltered, "I can do?"

Even if the words meant nothing, the offer must have touched him. "No, Jack," he answered quietly; "there is n't." With the words the hall door opened and Bucks, storm-beaten in his ulster, threw it wide and stood facing us both. The wind that swept in behind him blew out the lamps and left us in darkness.

"Jack, will you light up?"

It was Blackburn who spoke to me. But Bucks broke in instantly, speaking to him:

"Callahan called me over his house wire a few

minutes ago, Blackburn, and told me to meet him
here right away. Is anything wrong?" he asked,
with anxiety restrained in his tone.

I struck a match. I was so nervous that I took
hold of the hot chimney of the counter lamp
and dropped it smash to the floor. No one said
a word and that made me worse. I struck a
second match, and a third, and with a fourth got
the lamp on the despatchers' table lighted as Blackburn answered the superintendent. "Something
serious has happened," he replied to Bucks. "I
sent lap orders at one o'clock for Number One
and the Irving Special."

Bucks stared at him.

"Instead of making a meeting-point at O'Fallon's I sent One an order to run to O'Fallon's and
ordered the Special to run to Salt Rocks against
One."

"Why, my God!" exclaimed Bucks, "that
will bring them together in — the Peace cañon —
Blackburn! — Blackburn! — Blackburn!" he cried,
tearing off his storm-coat. He walked to the table,

seized the order book and steadied himself with one hand on the chair; I never saw him like that. But it looked as if the horror long averted, the trouble in the Peace River cañon, had come. The sleet tore at the old depot like a wolf, and with the sash shivering, Bucks turned like an executioner on his subordinate.

"What have you done to meet it?" He drew his watch, and his words came sharp as doom. "Where 's your wreckers? Where 's your relief? What have you done? What are you doing? *Nothing?* Why don't you speak? Will you kill two trainloads of people without an effort to do anything?"

His voice rang absolute terror to me; I looked toward Blackburn perfectly helpless.

"Bucks, there will be no wreck," he answered steadily.

"Be no wreck!" thundered Bucks, towering in the dingy room dark as the sweep of the wind. "Be no wreck? Two passenger trains meet in hell and be no wreck? Are you crazy?"

The despatcher's hands clutched at the table.
"No," he persisted steadily, "I am not crazy,
Bucks. Don't make me so. I tell you there will
not be a wreck."

Bucks, uncertain with amazement, stared at
him again.

"Blackburn, if you're sane I don't know what
you mean. Don't stand there like that. Do you
know what you have done?" The superintendent advanced toward him as he spoke; there was
a trace of pity in his words that seemed to open
Blackburn's pent heart more than all the bitterness.

"Bucks," he struggled, putting out a hand toward
his chief, "I am sure of what I say. There will
be no wreck. When I saw what I had done —
knew it was too late to undo it — I begged God
that my hands might not be stained with their
blood." Sweat oozed from the wretched man's
forehead. Every word wrung its bead of agony.
"I was answered," he exclaimed with a strange
confidence, "there will be no wreck. I cannot

see what will happen. I do not know what; but there will be no wreck, believe me or not — it is so."

His steadfast manner staggered the superintendent. I could imagine what he was debating as he looked at Blackburn — wondering, maybe, whether the man's mind was gone. Bucks was staggered; he looked it, and as he collected himself to speak again the hall door opened like an uncanny thing, and we all started as Callahan burst in on us.

" What's so? " he echoed. " What's up here? What did it mean, Blackburn? There's been trouble, has n't there? What's the matter with you all? Bucks? Is everybody struck dumb? "

Bucks spoke. " There's a lap order out on One and the theatrical Special, Callahan. We don't know what's happened," said Bucks sullenly. " Blackburn here has gone crazy — or he knows — somehow — there won't be any wreck," added the superintendent slowly and bewilderedly. " It's between O'Fallon's and Salt Rocks somewhere.

Callahan, take the key," he cried of a sudden.
"There's a call now. Despatcher! Don't speak;
ask no questions. Get that message," he exclaimed
sharply, pointing to the instrument. "It may be
news."

And it was news: news from Ames Station re-
porting the Irving Special *in* at 1.52 A. M. — out
at 1.54! We all heard it together, or it might
not have been believed. The Irving Special, eastbound, safely past Number One, westbound, on a
single track when their meeting orders had lapped!
Past without a word of danger or of accident, or
even that they had seen Number One and stopped
in time to avoid a collision? Exactly; not a word;
nothing. In at 52; out at 54. And the actors
hard asleep in the berths — and on about its business the Irving Special — that's what we got from
Ames.

Callahan looked around. "Gentlemen, what
does this mean? Somebody here is insane. I
don't know whether it's me or you, Blackburn.
Are you horsing me?" he exclaimed, raising his

voice angrily. "If you are, I want to say I con-
sider it a damned shabby joke."

Bucks put up a hand and without a word of
comment repeated Blackburn's story just as the
despatcher had told it. "In any event there's
nothing to do now; it's on us or we're past it.
Let us wait for Number One to report."

Callahan pored over the order book. "Maybe," he asked after a while, "did n't you send the
orders right and copy them wrong in the book,
Blackburn?"

The despatcher shook his head. "They went
as they stand. The orders lapped, Callahan.
Wait till we hear from Number One. I feel
sure she is safe. Wait."

Bucks was pacing the floor. Callahan stuck silent
to the key, taking what little work came, for I saw
neither of the chiefs wanted to trust Blackburn at
the key. He sat, looking, for the most part, vacantly
into the fire. Callahan meantime had the orders
repeated back from Ames and Rosebud. It was
as Blackburn had said; they did lap; they had been

sent just as the order book showed. There was
nothing for it but to wait for Rosebud to hear
from Number One. When the night operator
there called the despatcher again it brought Blackburn out of his gloom like a thunderclap.

" Give me the key ! " he exclaimed. " There
is Rosebud." Callahan pushed back and Blackburn, dropping into the chair, took the message
from the night operator at Rosebud.

" Number One, in, 2.03 A. M."

Blackburn answered him, and strangely, with all
the easy confidence of his ordinary sending. He
sat and took and sent like one again master of the
situation.

" Ask Engineer Sampson to come to the wire,"
said he to Rosebud. Sampson, not Maje, but his
brother Arnold, was pulling Number One that
night.

" Engineer Sampson here," came from Rosebud
presently.

" Ask Sampson where he met Special 202
to-night."

We waited, wrought up, for in that reply must come the answer to all the mystery. There was a hitch at the other end of the wire; then Rosebud answered:

"Sampson says he will tell you all about it in the morning."

"That will not do," tapped the despatcher. "This is Blackburn. Superintendent Bucks and Callahan are here. They want the facts. Where did you meet Special 202?"

There was another wearing delay. When the answer came it was slowly, at the engineer's dictation.

"My orders were to hold at O'Fallon's for Special 202," clicked the sounder, repeating the engineer's halting statement. "When we cleared Salt Rocks siding and got down among the Quakers, I was cutting along pretty hard to make the cañon when I saw, or thought I saw, a headlight flash between the buttes across the river. It startled me, for I knew the 202 Special could not be very far west of us. Anyway, I made a quick

stop, and reversed and backed tight as I could make
it for Salt Rocks siding.   Before we had got a
mile I saw the headlight again, and I knew the 202
was against our order.   We got into the clear just
as the Special went by humming.   Nobody but our
train crew and my fireman knows anything about
this."

The three men in front of me made no comment
as they looked at each other.   How was it possible
for one train to have seen the headlight of another
among the buttes of the Peace River country ?

It was — possible.   Just possible.   But to figure
once in how many times a vista would have opened
for a single second so one engineer could see the
light of another would stagger a multiplying machine.
Chance ?   Well, yes, perhaps.   But there were no
suggestions of that nature that night under the despatcher's lamp at the Wickiup, with the storm driv-
ing down the pass as it drove that night; and yet
at Peace River, where the clouds never rested, that
night was clear.   Blackburn, getting up, steadied
himself on his feet.

"Go in there and lie down," said Callahan to
him. "You 're used up, old fellow, I can see that.
I 'll take the key. Don't say a word."

"Not a word, Blackburn," put in Bucks, resting his big hand on the despatcher's shoulder.
"There 's no harm done; nobody knows it. Bury
the thing right here to-night. You 're broke up.
Go in there and lie down."

He took their hands; started to speak; but they
pushed him into Callahan's room; they did n't want
to hear anything.

All the night it stormed at the Wickiup. In
the morning the Irving Special, flying toward Chicago, was far down the Platte. Number One was
steaming west, deep in the heart of the Rockies;
Blackburn lay in Callahan's room. It was nine
o'clock, and the sun was streaming through the
east windows when Fred Norman opened the office
door. Fred could do those things even when he
was sickest. Have a hemorrhage one day, scare
everybody to death, and go back to his trick the
next. He asked right away for Kit, as he called

Blackburn, and when they pointed to Callahan's
door Fred pushed it open and went in. A cry
brought the operators to him. Blackburn was
stretched on his knees half on the floor, half face
downward on the sofa. His head had fallen between his arms, which were stretched above it.   In
his hands, clasped tight, they found his watch with
the picture of his wife and his baby.   Had he asked,
when he first went into that room that night — when
he wrestled like Jacob of old in his agony of prayer
— that his life be taken if only their lives, the lives
of those in his keeping, might be spared ?   I do not
know.   They found him dead.

Held for Orders

❧

The Nightman's Story

❧

BULLHEAD

The Nightman's Story

BULLHEAD

HIS full name was James Gillespie Blaine
Lyons; but his real name was Bullhead
— just plain Bullhead.

When he began passenger braking the trainmaster put him on with Pat Francis. The very
first trip he made, a man in the smoking car asked
him where the drinking water was. Bullhead,
though sufficiently gaudy in his new uniform, was
not prepared for any question that might be thrown
at him. He pulled out his book of rules, which
he had been told to consult in case of doubt, and
after some study referred his inquirer to the fire-
bucket hanging at the front end of the car. The

passenger happened to be a foreigner and very thirsty. He climbed up on the Baker heater, according to directions, and did at some risk get hold of the bucket — but it was empty.

"Iss no vater hier," cried the second-class man. Bullhead sat half way back in the car, still studying the rules. He looked up surprised but turning around pointed with confidence to the firepail at the hind end of the smoker.

"Try the other bucket, Johnnie," he said, calmly. At that every man in the car began to choke; and the German, thinking the new brakeman was making funny of him, wanted to fight. Now Bullhead would rather fight than go to Sunday-school any day, and without parley he engaged the insulted homesteader. Pat Francis parted them after some hard words on his part; and Kenyon, the trainmaster, gave Bullhead three months to study up where the water cooler was located in Standard, A pattern, smoking cars. Bullhead's own mother, who did Callahan's washing, refused to believe her son was so stupid as not to know; but

Bullhead, who now tells the story himself, claims
he did not know.

When he got back to work he tried the freight
trains. They put him on the Number Twenty-
nine, local, and one day they were drifting into the
yard at Goose River Junction when there came
from the cab a sharp call for brakes. Instead of
climbing out and grabbing a brakewheel for dear
life, Bullhead looked out the window to see what
the excitement was. By the time he had decided
what rule covered the emergency his train had
driven a stray flat half way through the eating
house east of the depot. Kenyon, after hearing
Bullhead's own candid statement of fact, coughed
apologetically and said three years; whereupon
Bullhead resigned permanently from the train
service and applied for a job in the roundhouse.

But the roundhouse — for a boy like Bullhead.
It would hardly do. He was put at helping Pete
Beezer, the boiler washer. One night Pete was
snatching his customary nap in the pit when the
hose got away from Bullhead and struck his boss.

In the confusion, Peter, who was nearly drowned, lost a set of teeth; that was sufficient in that department of the motive power; Bullhead moved on, suddenly. Neighbor thought he might do for a wiper. After the boy had learned something about wiping he tried one day to back an engine out on the turntable just to see whether it was easy. It was; dead easy; but the turntable happened to be arranged wrong for the experiment; and Neighbor, before calling in the wrecking gang, took occasion to kick Bullhead out of the roundhouse bodily.

Nevertheless, Bullhead, like every Medicine Bend boy, wanted to railroad. Some fellows can't be shut off. He was offered the presidency of a Cincinnati bank by a private detective agency which had just sent up the active head of the institution for ten years; but as Bullhead could not arrange transportation east of the river he was obliged to let the opportunity pass.

When the widow Lyons asked Callahan to put Jamie at telegraphing the assistant superintendent nearly fell off his chair. Mrs. Lyons, however,

was in earnest, as the red-haired man soon found
by the way his shirts were starched.   Her son,
meantime, had gotten hold of a sounder, and was
studying telegraphy, corresponding at the same
time with the Cincinnati detective agency for the
town and county rights to all " hidden and undis-
covered crime," on the Mountain Division — rights
offered at the very reasonable price of ten dollars
by registered mail, bank draft or express money
order; currency at sender's risk.   The only obli-
gations imposed by this deal were secrecy and a
German silver star; and Bullhead, after holding
his trusting mother up for the ten, became a regularly installed detective with proprietary rights to
local misdeeds.   Days he plied his sounder, and
nights he lay awake trying to mix up Pete Beezer
and Neighbor with the disappearance of various
bunches of horses from the Bar M ranch.

About the same time he became interested in
dentistry ; not that there is any obvious connection between railroading and detective work and
filling teeth — but his thoughts just turned that

way and following the advice of a local dentist, who did n't want altogether to discourage him, Bullhead borrowed a pair of forceps and pulled all the teeth out of a circular saw to get his arm into practice. Before the dentist pronounced him proficient, though, his mother had Callahan reduced to terms, and the assistant superintendent put Bullhead among the operators.

That was a great day for Bullhead. He had to take the worst of it, of course; sweeping the office and that; but whatever his faults, the boy did as he was told. Only one vicious habit clung to him — he had a passion for reading the rules. In spite of this, however, he steadily mastered the taking, and, as for sending, he could do that before he got out of the cuspidor department. Everybody around the Wickiup bullied him, and maybe that was his salvation. He got used to expecting the worst of it, and nerved himself to take it, which in railroading is half the battle.

A few months after he became competent to handle a key the nightman at Goose River Junction went wrong. When Callahan told Bullhead he thought about giving him the job, the boy went wild with excitement, and in a burst of confidence showed Callahan his star. It was the best thing that ever happened, for the assistant head of the division had an impulsive way of swearing the nonsense out of a boy's head, and when Bullhead confessed to being a detective a fiery stream was poured on him. The foolishness couldn't quite all be driven out in one round; but Jamie Lyons went to Goose River fairly well informed as to how much of a fool he was.

Goose River Junction is not a lively place. It has been claimed that even the buzzards at Goose River Junction play solitaire. But apart from the utter loneliness it was hard to hold operators there on account of Nellie Cassidy. A man rarely stayed at Goose River past the second pay-check. When he got money enough to resign he resigned; and all because Nellie Cassidy despised operators.

The lunch counter that Matt Cassidy, Nellie's father, ran at the Junction was just an adjunct for feeding train crews and the few miners who wandered down from the Glencoe spur. Matt himself took the night turn, but days it was Nellie who heated the Goose River coffee and dispensed the pie — contract pie made at Medicine Bend, and sent by local freight classified as ammunition, loaded and released, O. R.

It was Nellie's cruelty that made the frequent shifts at Goose River. Not that she was unimpressible, or had no heroes. She had plenty of them in the engine and the train service. It was the smart-uniformed young conductors and the kerchiefed juvenile engineers on the fast runs to whom Nellie paid deference, and for whom she served the preferred doughnuts.

But this was nothing to Bullhead. He had his head so full of things when he took his new position that he failed to observe Nellie's contempt. He was just passing out of the private detective stage ; just getting over dental beginnings ; just rising to the responsibility of the key, and a month devoted to his immediate work and the study of the rules passed like a limited train. Previous to the coming of Bullhead, no Goose River man had tried study of the rules as a remedy for loneliness; it proved a great scheme; but it aroused the un-measured contempt of Nellie Cassidy. She scorned Bullhead unspeakably, and her only uneasiness was that he seemed unconscious of it.

However, the little Goose River girl had no idea of letting him escape that way. When scorn became clearly useless she tried cajolery — she smiled on Bullhead. Not till then did he give up; her smile was his undoing. It was so absolutely novel to Bullhead — Bullhead, who had never got anything but kicks and curses and frowns. Before Nellie's smiles, judiciously administered, Bullhead melted like the sugar she began to sprinkle in his coffee. That was what she wanted; when he was fairly dissolved, Nellie like the coffee went gradually cold. Bullhead became miserable, and to her life at Goose River was once more endurable.

It was then that Bullhead began to sit up all

day, after working all night, to get a single smile
from the direction of the pie rack. He hung,
utterly miserable, around the lunch room all day,
while Nellie made impersonal remarks about the
colorless life of a mere operator as compared with
life in the cab of a ten-wheeler. She admired the
engineer, Nellie — was there ever a doughnut girl
who did n't? And when One or Two rose smoking out of the alkali east or the alkali west, and the
mogul engine checked its gray string of sleepers at
the Junction platform, and Bat Mullen climbed
down to oil 'round — as he always did — there
were the liveliest kind of heels behind the counter.

Such were the moments when Bullhead sat in
the lunch room, unnoticed, somewhat back where
the flies were bad, and helped himself aimlessly
to the sizzling maple syrup — Nellie rustling back
and forth for Engineer Mullen, who ran in for a
quick cup, and consulted, after each swallow, a
dazzling open-faced gold watch, thin as a double
eagle; for Bat at twenty-one was pulling the fast
trains and carried the best. And with Bullhead

feeding on flannel cakes and despair, and Nellie
Cassidy looking quite her smartest, Mullen would
drink his coffee in an impassive rush, never even
glancing Bullhead's way — absolutely ignoring
Bullhead.   What was he but a nightman, anyway ?
Then Mullen would take as much as a minute of
his running time to walk forward to the engine
with Miss Cassidy, and stand in the lee of the
drivers chatting with her, while Bullhead went
completely frantic.

It was being ignored in that way, after her smiles
had once been his, that crushed the night operator.
It filled his head with schemes for obtaining recog-
nition at all hazards.   He began by quarrelling violently with Nellie, and things were coming to a
serious pass around the depot when the Klondike
business struck the Mountain Division.   It came
with a rush and when they began running through
freight extras by way of the Goose River short
line, day and night, the Junction station caught the
thick of it.   It was something new altogether for
the short line rails and the short line operators, and

Bullhead's night trick, with nothing to do but poke the fire and pop at coyotes, became straightway a busy and important post. The added work kept him jumping from sundown till dawn, and kept him from loafing daytimes around the lunch counter and ruining himself on fermented syrup.

On a certain night, windier than all the November nights that had gone before, the night operator sat alone in the office facing a resolve. Goose River had become intolerable. Medicine Bend was not to be thought of, for Bullhead now had a suspicion, due to Callahan, that he was a good deal of a chump, and he wanted to get away from the ridicule that had always and everywhere made life a burden. There appeared to Bullhead nothing for it but the Klondike. On the table before the moody operator lay his letter of resignation, addressed in due form to J. S. Bucks, superintendent. Near it, under the lamp, lay a well-thumbed copy of the book of rules, open at the chapter on Resignations, with subheads on —

Resign, who should.

Resign, how to.

Resign, when to.   (See also Time.)

The fact was it had at last painfully forced itself
on Bullhead that he was not fitted for the railroad
business.   Pat Francis had unfeelingly told him so.
Callahan had told him so; Neighbor had told him
so; Bucks had told him so.   On that point the lead-
ing West End authorities were agreed.   Yet in
spite of these discouragements he had persisted and
at last made a show.   Who was it now that had
shaken his stubborn conviction?   Bullhead hardly
dared confess.   But it was undoubtedly one who
put up to be no authority whatever on Motive
Power or Train Service or Operating — it was
Matt Cassidy's girl.

While he reread his formal letter and compared
on spelling with his pocket Webster, a train whistled.   Bullhead looked at the clock: 11.40 P. M.
It was the local freight, Thirty, coming in from the
West, working back to Medicine.   From the East,
Number One had not arrived; she was six hours
late, and Bullhead looked out at his light, for he

had orders for the freight. It was not often that such a thing happened, because One rarely went off schedule badly enough to throw her into his turn. He had his orders copied and O.K.'d, and waited only to deliver them.

It was fearfully windy. The 266 engine, pulling Thirty that night, wheezed in the gale like a man with the apoplexy. She had a new fireman on, who was burning the life out of her, and as she puffed painfully down on the scrap rails of the first siding and took the Y, her overloaded safety gasped violently.

When the conductor of the Number Thirty train opened the station door, the wind followed him like a catamount. The stove puffed open with a down draft, and shot the room full of stinging smoke. The lamp blaze flew up the chimney — out — and left the nightman and the conductor in darkness. The trainman with a swear shoved-to the door, and Bullhead, the patient, turned over his letter of resignation quick in the dark, felt for a match and relighted his lamp. Swearing again at

Bullhead, the freight conductor swaggered over to his table, felt in all the operator's pockets for a cigar, tumbled all the papers around, and once more, on general principles, swore.

Bullhead took things uncomplainingly, but he watched close, and was determined to fight if the brute discovered his letter of resignation. When the trainman could think of no further indignities he took his orders, to meet Number One at Sackley, the second station east of Goose River. After he had signed, Bullhead asked him about the depot fire at Bear Dance that had been going over the wires for two hours, reminded him of the slow order for the number nine culvert and as the rude visitor slammed the door behind him, held his hand over the lamp. Then he sat down again and turned over his letter of resignation.

To make it binding it lacked only his signature — James Gillespie Blaine Lyons — now, himself, of the opinion of every one else on the West End: that he was just a natural born blooming fool. He lifted his pen to sign off the aspirations of a young lifetime when the sounder began to snap and sputter his call. It was the despatcher, and he asked hurriedly if Number Thirty was there.

"Number Thirty is on the Y," answered Bull-head.

Then came a train order. "Hold Number Thirty till Number One arrives."

Bullhead repeated the order, and got back the O. K. He grabbed his hat and hurried out of the door to deliver the new order to the local freight before it should pull out.

To reach the train Bullhead had to cross the short line tracks. The wind was scouring the flats, and as he tacked up the platform the dust swept dead into him. At the switch he sprang across the rails, thinking of nothing but reaching the engine cab of the local — forgetting about the track he was crossing. Before he could think or see or jump, a through freight on the short line, wild, from the West, storming down the grade behind him, struck Bullhead as a grizzly would a gnat — hurled him, doubling, fifty feet out on the spur — and stormed on into the East without a quiver out of the ordinary. One fatality followed another. The engineer of the short line train did not see the man he had hit, and with the night-man lying unconscious in the ditch, the local freight pulled out for Sackley.

Bullhead never knew just how long he lay under the stars. When his head began to whirl the wind was blowing cool and strong on him, and the alkali dust was eddying into his open mouth. It was only a matter of seconds, though it seemed hours, to pull himself together and to put up his hand unsteadily to feel what it was soaking warm and sticky into his hair; then to realize that he had been struck by a short line train; to think of what a failure he had lately acknowl-edged himself to be; and of what it was he was clutching so tightly in his right hand — the holding order for Number Thirty. He raised his reeling head; there was a drift of starlight through the dust cloud, but no train in sight; Number Thirty was gone. With that consciousness came a recollection — he had forgotten to put out his red light.

His red light was n't out. He kept repeating that to himself to put the picture of what it meant before him. He had started to deliver an order without putting out his light, and Number Thirty was gone; against Number One — a head end collision staring the freight and the belated passenger in the face. Number Thirty, running hard on her order to make Sackley for the meeting, and One, running furiously, as she always ran — to-night worse than ever.

He lifted his head, enraged with himself; enraged. He thought about the rules, and he grew enraged. Only himself he blamed, nobody else — studying the rules for a lifetime and just when it would mean the death of a trainload of people forgetting his red signal. He lifted his head; it was sick, deadly sick. But up it must come, Thirty gone, and it wabbled, swooning sick and groggy as he stared around and tried to locate himself. One thing he could see, the faint outline of the station and his lamp blazing smoky in the window. Bullhead figured a second; then he began to crawl. If he could reach the lamp before his head went off again, before he went completely silly, he might yet save himself and Number One.

It was n't in him to crawl till he thought of his own mistake; but there was a spur in the sweep of that through his head. His brain, he knew, was wabbling, but he could crawl; and he stuck fainting to that one idea, and crawled for the light of his lamp.

It is a bare hundred feet across to the Y. Bullhead taped every foot of the hundred with blood. There was no one to call on for help; he just stuck to the crawl, grinding his teeth in bitter self-reproach. They traced him, next morning when he was past the telling of it, and his struggle looked the track of a wounded bear. Dragging along one crushed leg and half crazed by the crack on his forehead, Bullhead climbed to the platform, across, and dragged himself to the door. He can tell yet about rolling his broken leg under him and raising himself to grasp the thumb latch. Not until he tried to open it did he remember it was a spring lock and that he was outside. He felt in his pocket for his keys — but his keys were gone.

There were no rules to consult then. No way on earth of getting into the office in time to do anything; to drag himself to the lunch room, twice further than the station, was out of the question. But there was a way to reach his key in spite of all bad things, and Bullhead knew the way. He struggled fast around to the window. Raising himself with a frightful twinge on one knee, he beat at the glass with his fist. Clutching the sash, he drew himself up with a hand, and with the other tore away the muntin, stuck his head and shoulders through the opening, got his hand on the key, and called the first station east, Blaisdell, with the 19. Life and death that call meant; the 19, the despatcher's call — hanging over the key, stammering the 19 over the wire, and baptizing the call in his own blood — that is the way Bullhead learned to be a railroad man.

For Blaisdell got him and his warning, and had Number One on the siding just as the freight tore around the west curve, headed for Sackley. While it was all going on, Bullhead lay on the wind-swept platform at Goose River with a hole in his head that would have killed anybody on the West End, or, for that matter on earth except James Gillespie Blaine Lyons.

After Number Thirty had passed so impudently, Number One felt her way rather cautiously to Goose River, because the despatchers could n't get the blamed station.   They decided, of course, that Bullhead was asleep, and fixed everything at the Wickiup to send a new man up there on Three in the morning and fire him for good.

But about one o'clock Number One rolled, bad-tempered, into Goose River Junction, and Bat Mullen, stopping his train, strode angrily to the station. It was dark as a pocket inside. Bat smashed in the door with his heel, and the train-

men swarmed in and began looking with their lanterns for the nightman.   The stove was red-hot,
but he was not asleep in the arm-chair, nor nap-
ping under the counter on the supplies.   They
turned to his table and discovered the broken window, and thought of a hold-up.   They saw where
the nightman had spilled something that looked
like ink over the table, over the order book, over
the clip, and there was a hand print that looked
inky on an open letter addressed to the superintendent — and a little pool of something like ink
under the key.

Somebody said suicide; but Bat Mullen suddenly stuck his lamp out of the broken window,
put his head through after it, and cried out.   Setting his lantern down on the platform, he crawled
through the broken sash and picked up Bullhead.

Next morning it was all over the West End.

"And Bullhead!" cried everybody.   "That's
what gets me.   Who'd have thought it of *Bullhead!*"

When they all got up there and saw what Bull-

head had done, everybody agreed that nobody but
Bullhead could have done it.

The pilot bar of the short line mogul, in swip-
ing Bullhead unmercifully, had really made a railroad man of him. It had let a great light in on
the situation. Whereas before every one else on
the line had been to blame for his failures, Bullhead now saw that he himself had been to blame,
and was man enough to stand up and say so.
When the big fellows, Callahan and Kenyon and
Pat Francis, saw his trail next morning, saw the
blood smeared over the table, and saw Bullhead's
letter of resignation signed in his own blood man-
ual, and heard his straight-out story days afterward, they said never a word.

But that morning, the morning after, Callahan
picked up the letter and put it just as it was between the leaves of the order book and locked both
in his grip. It was some weeks before he had a
talk with Bullhead, and he spoke then only a few
words, because the nightman fainted before he got
through. Callahan made him understand, though,

that as soon as he was able he could have any key on that division he wanted as long as *he* was running it — and Callahan is running that division yet.

It all came easy after he got well. Instead of getting the worst of it from everybody, Bullhead began to get the best of it, even from pretty Nellie Cassidy. But Nellie had missed her opening. She tried tenderness while the boy was being nursed at the Junction. Bullhead looked grim and far-off through his bulging bandages, and asked his mother to put the sugar in his coffee for him ; Bullhead was getting sense.

Besides, what need has a young man with a heavy crescent-shaped scar on his forehead, that people inquire about and who within a year after the Goose River affair was made a train despatcher under Barnes Tracy at Medicine Bend — what need has he of a coquette's smiles ? His mother, who has honorably retired from hard work, says half the girls at the Bend are after him, and his mother ought to know, for she keeps house for him.

Bullhead's letter of resignation with the print of his hand on it hangs framed over Callahan's desk, and is shown to railroad big fellows who are accorded the courtesies of the Wickiup.   But when they ask Bullhead about it, he just laughs and says some railroad men have to have sense pounded into them.

Held for Orders

The Master Mechanic's Story

DELAROO

The Master Mechanic's Story

DELAROO

"YOU TELL IT. I can't tell it," growled Neighbor.

"Oh, no. No. That's your story, Neighbor."

"I ain't no story-teller — "

"Just an able-jawed liar," suggested Callahan through a benevolent bluish haze.

"Delaroo's story was n't any lie, though," muttered Neighbor. "But a fellow would think it was to hear it; now he would, for a fact, would n't he?"

I

IF you want him, quick and short, it would be : whiskers, secret societies, statistics and plug tobacco — the latter mostly worked up. That was Maje Sampson.

Bluntly, a wind-bag; two hundred and seventy pounds of atmosphere. Up on benevolent fraternities, up on politics, up on the money question, up on everything. The Seven Financial Conspiracies engaged Maje Sampson's attention pretty continually, and had for him a practical application : there were never less than seven conspiracies afoot in Medicine Bend to make Maje Sampson pay up.

Pay ? Indeed, he did pay. He was always paying. It was not a question of paying. Not at all. It was a question of paying up, which is different.

The children — they were brickbats. Towheaded, putty-faced, wash-eyed youngsters of all sizes and conditions. About Maje Sampson's children there was but one distinguishing characteristic, they were all boys, nothing but boys, and they spread all over town.   Was there a baby run over? It was Maje Sampson's.   Was there a child lost? Maje Sampson's.   Was there a violently large-headed, coarse-featured, hangdog, clattering sort of a chap anywhere around?   In the street, station, roundhouse, yards, stock pens?   It was a brick-bat, sure, one of Maje Sampson's brickbat boys.

The Sampsons were at the end of the street, and the end of the street was up the mountain.   Maje Sampson's lot, " raired," as Neighbor put it — stood on its hind legs.   His house had a startling tumble-over aspect as you approached it.   The back end of his lot ran up into the sheer, but he marked the line sharply by a kind of horizontal fence, because the cliff just above belonged to the corporation that owned everything else on earth around Medicine Bend.

Maje Sampson did not propose to let any grasp-ing corporation encroach on his lines, so he built, and added to from time to time, a cluster of things on the hind end of his lot — an eruption of small buildings like pimples on a boy's nose, running down in size from the barn to the last drygoods box the boys had heaved up the slope for a dog house.   To add to the variety, some one of the structures was always getting away in the wind, and if anything smaller than a hotel was seen careening across-lots in a Medicine Bend breeze it was spotted without further investigation as Maje Sampson's.   When the gale abated, Joe McBracken, who conducted the local dray line, was pretty sure to be seen with a henhouse or a woodshed, or something likewise, loaded on his trucks headed for Maje Sampson's. Once the whole lean-to of the house blew off, but Joe McBracken stood ready for any emergency. He met the maverick addition at the foot of the grade, loaded it on his house-moving truck, hitched on four bronchos, crawled inside the structure, and, getting the lines through the front window, drove up Main Street before the wind had gone down. Joe was photographed in the act, and afterward used the exhibit in getting judgment against Maje Sampson for his bill.

Now a man like Maje would n't be likely to have very much of a run nor very much of an engine. He had the 264; an old pop bottle with a stack like a tepee turned upside down. For a run he had always trains Number Twenty-nine and Thirty, the local freights, with an accommodation coach east of Anderson. There were times of stress frequently on the West End, times when everybody ran first in first out, except Maje Sampson; he always ran Twenty-nine and Thirty west to Silver River and back. A pettifogging, cheap, jerk-water run with no rights to speak of, not even against respectable hand-cars. The only things Maje Sampson did not have to dodge were tramps, blanket Indians and telegraph poles; everything else side-tracked Twenty-nine and Thirty and Maje Sampson. Almost everybody on through trains must at some time have seen Maje Sampson puffing on a siding as Moore or Mullen shot by on Number One or Number Two. Maje was so big and his cab so little that when he got his head through the window you could n't see very much of

the cab for shoulders and whiskers and things.
From the cab window he looked like a fourteen-
year-old boy springing out of a ten-year-old jacket.
Three things only, made Maje tolerable. First,
the number of benevolent orders he belonged to ;
second, Delaroo ; third, Martie.

Maje Sampson was a joiner and a sitter up. He
would join anything on the West End that had
a ritual, a grip and a password, and he would sit up
night after night with anybody that had a broken
leg or a fever : and if nothing better offered, Maje,
rather than go to bed, would tackle a man with the
stomachache. This kind of took the cuss off ; but
he was that peculiar he would sit up all night with
a sick man and next day make everybody sick talking
the money question — at least everybody but
Delaroo. If Delaroo was bored he never showed
it. As long as Maje would talk Delaroo would
listen. That single word was in fact the key to
Delaroo : Delaroo was a listener ; for that reason
nobody knew much about him.

He was n't a railroad man by birth, but by

adoption.   Delaroo came from the mountains : he
was just a plain mountain man.   Some said his
father was a trapper ; if so, it explained everything
— the quiet, the head bent inquiringly forward, the
modest unobtrusiveness of a man deaf.   Of a size
and shape nothing remarkable, Delaroo — but a
great listener, for though he looked like a deaf
man he heard like a despatcher, and saw mar-
vellously from out the ends of his silent eyes.
Delaroo for all the world was a trapper.

He came into the service as a roundhouse
sweeper ; then Neighbor, after a long time, put
him at wiping.   Delaroo said nothing but wiped
for years and years, and was in a fair way to become liked, when, instead, he became one morning
pitted with umbilical vesicles, and the doctors, with
Delaroo's brevity, said smallpox.   The boarding
house keeper threw him out bodily and at once.
Having no better place to go, Delaroo wandered into
Steve Boyer's saloon, where he was generally wel-
come.   Steve, however, pointed a hospitable gun at
him and suggested his getting away immediately

from the front end of it. Delaroo went from there to the roundhouse with his umbilicals, and asked Neighbor what a man with the smallpox ought to do with it. Neighbor would n't run, not even from the smallpox — but he told Delaroo what it meant to get the smallpox started in the round-house, and Delaroo wandered quietly away from the depot grounds, a pretty sick man then, stag-gered up the yards, and crawled stupid into a box car to die without embarrassing anybody.

By some hook or crook, nobody to this day knows how, that car was switched on to Maje Sampson's train when it was made up that day for the West. Maybe it was done as a trick to scare the wind-bag engineer. If so, the idea was suc-cessful. When the hind-end brakeman at the second stop came forward and reported a tramp with the smallpox in the empty box car, Maje was angry. But his curiosity gradually got the upper hand. This man might be, by some distant chance, he reflected, a P. Q. W. of A., or a frater, or a fellow, or a knight or something like — and when they stopped again to throw off crackers and beer and catsup, Maje went back and entered the infected car like a lion-tamer to try lodge signals and things on him.   Maje advanced and gave the countersign.   It was not cordially received.   He tried another and another — and another ; his passes were lost in the air.   The smallpox man appeared totally unable to come back at Maje with anything.   He was not only delirious, but by this time so frightfully broken out that Maje could n't have touched a sound spot with a Masonic signal of distress. Finally the venturesome engineer walked closer into the dark corner where the sick man lay — and by Heaven! it was the Indian wiper, Delaroo.

When Maje Sampson got back into the cab he could not speak — at least not for publication. He was tearing mad and sputtered like a safety. He gathered up his cushion and a water bottle and a bottle that would explode if water touched it, and crawled with his plunder into the box car. He straightened Delaroo up and out and gave him a drink and by way of sanitary precaution took one personally, for he himself had never had the smallpox — but once. When he had done this little for Delaroo he finished his run and came back to the Bend hauling his pest-house box car. The fireman quit the cab immediately after Maje exposed himself; the conductor communicated with him only by signals. The Anderson operator wired ahead that Maje Sampson was bringing back a man with smallpox on Thirty, and when Maje, bulging out of the 264 cab, pulled into the division yard nobody would come within a mile of him. He set out the box car below the stock pens, cross-lots from his house up on the hill, and, not being able to get advice from anybody else, went home to consult Martie.

Though there were a great many women in Medicine Bend, Maje Sampson looked to but one, Martie, the little washed-out woman up at Sampson's — wife, mother, nurse, cook, slave — Martie.

No particular color hair; no particular color eyes; no particular color gown; no particular cut to it. A plain bit of a woman, mother of six boys, large and small, and wife of a great big wind-bag engineer, big as three of her by actual measurement. By the time Maje had taken counsel and walked down town prominent business men were fending off his approach with shotguns. The city marshal from behind a bomb-proof asked what he was going to do with his patient, and Maje retorted he was going to take him home. He was n't a M. R. W. of T. nor a P. S. G. of W. E., but he was a roundhouse man, and between Maje and a railroad man, a wiper even, there was a bond stronger than grip or password or jolly business of any kind. The other things Maje, without realizing it, merely played at; but as to the railroad lay — if a railroad man was the right sort he could borrow anything the big fellow had, money, plug tobacco, pipe, water bottle, strong bottle, it made no odds what. And, on the other hand, Maje would n't hesitate to borrow any or all of these things in return; the railroad man who got ahead of Maje Sampson in this respect had claims to be considered a past grand in the business.

The doughty engineer lifted and dragged and hauled Delaroo home with him. If there was no hospital, Martie had said, no pest house, no nothing, just bring him home. They had all had the smallpox up at Sampson's except the baby, and the doctor had said lately the baby appeared to need something. They had really everything up at Sampson's sooner or later : measles, diphtheria, croup, everything on earth except money. And Martie Sampson, with the washing and mending and scrubbing and cooking, nursed the outcast wiper through his smallpox. The baby took it, of course, and Martie nursed the baby through and went on just the same as before — washing, mending, cooking, scrubbing. Delaroo when he got well went to firing; Neighbor offered the job as a kind of consolation prize ; and he went to firing on the 264 for Maje Sampson.

It was then that Maje took Delaroo fairly in hand and showed him the unspeakable folly of trying to get through the world without the comradeship and benefits of the B. S. L.'s of U., and the fraters of the order of the double-barrelled star of MacDuff.   Delaroo caught a good deal of it on the sidings, where they lay most of their time dodging first-class trains ; and evenings when they got in from their runs Delaroo, having nowhere else to go, used to wander, after supper, up to Sampson's. At Sampson's he would sit in the shade of the lamp and smoke while Maje, in his shirt-sleeves, held forth on the benevolent orders, and one boy crawled through the bowels of the organ and another pulled off the tablecloth — Delaroo always saving the lamp — and a third harassed the dog, and a fourth stuck pins in a fifth — and Martie, sitting on the dim side of the shade, so the operation would not appear too glaring, mended at Maje's mammoth trousers.

Delaroo would sit and listen to Maje and watch the heave of the organ with the boy, and the current of the tablecloth with the lamp, and the quarter in which the dog was chewing the baby, and watch Martie's perpetual-motion fingers for a whole evening, and go back to the boarding-house without passing a word with anybody on earth, he was that silent.

In this way the big, bluffing engineer gradually worked Delaroo into all the secret benevolent orders in Medicine Bend — that meant pretty much every one on earth. There arose always, however, in connection with the initiations of Delaroo one hitch : he never seemed quite to know whom he wanted to leave his insurance money to. He could go the most complicated catechism without a hitch every time, for Maje spent weeks on the sidings drilling him, until it came to naming the beneficiary ; there he stuck. Nobody could get out of him to whom he wanted his money to go.

Had he no relations back in the mountains ? Nobody up in the Spider country ? No wives or daughters or fathers or mothers or friends or anything ? Delaroo always shook his head. If they persisted he shook his head. Maje Sampson, sitting after supper, would ask, and Martie, when the dishes were side-tracked, would begin to sew and listen, and Delaroo, of course, would listen, but never by any chance would he answer; not even when Maje tried to explain how it bore on 16 to 1. He declined to discuss any ratio or to name any beneficiary whatsoever. The right honorable recording secretaries fumed and denounced it as irregular, and Maje Sampson wore holes in his elbows gesticulating, but in the matter of distributing his personal share of the unearned increment, Delaroo expressed no preference whatsoever. He paid his dues; he made his passes; he sat in his place, what more could be required? If they put him in a post of honor he filled it with a silent dignity. If they set him to guard the outer portal he guarded well; it was perilous rather for a visiting frater or even a local brother to try getting past Delaroo if he was rusty in the ritual. Not Maje Sampson himself could work the outer guard without the countersign; if he forgot it in the hurry of getting to lodge he had to cool his heels in the outer air till it came back; Delaroo was pitiless.

In the cab he was as taciturn as he was in the lodge or under the kerosene lamp at Sampson's; he just listened. But his firing was above any man's who ever stoked the 264. Delaroo made more steam on less coal than any man in the roundhouse. Neighbor began to hold him up as a model for the division, and the boys found that the way to jolly Neighbor was to say nice things about Delaroo. The head of the Motive Power would brighten out of a sulk at the mention of Delaroo's name, and he finally fixed up a surprise for the Indian man. One night after Delaroo came in, Neighbor, in the bluff way he liked to use in promoting a man, told Delaroo he could have an engine; a good one, one of the K. class; as much finer a machine than the old 264 as Duffy's chronometer was than a prize package watch. Delaroo never said ay, yes, or no; he merely listened. Neighbor never had a promotion received in just that way; it nearly gave him the apoplexy.

But if Delaroo treated the proposal coolly, not so Maje Sampson; when the news of the offer reached him, Maje went into an unaccountable flutter. He acted at first exactly as if he wanted to hold his man back, which was dead against cab ethics. Finally he assented, but his cheeks went flabby and his eyes hollow, and he showed more worry than his creditors. Nobody understood it, yet there was evidently something on, and the Major's anxiety increased until Delaroo, the Indian fireman and knight companion of the Ancient Order of Druids and Fluids, completely took Neighbor's breath by declining the new engine. That was a West End wonder. He said if it made no odds he would stay on the 264. The men all wondered; then something new came up and the thing was forgotten. Maje Sampson's cheeks filled out again, he regained his usual nerve, and swore on the money question harder than ever.

After that it was pretty generally understood that Delaroo and Maje Sampson and the 264 were fixtures. Neighbor never gave any one a chance to decline an engine more than once. The boys all knew, if Delaroo did n't, that he would be firing a long time after throwing that chance by; and he was.

The combination came to be regarded as eternal. When the sloppy 264 hove in sight, little Delaroo and big Maje Sampson were known to be behind the boiler pounding up and down the mountains, up and down, year in and year out. Big engines came into the division and bigger. All the time the division was crowding on the Motive Power and putting in the mammoth types, until, when the 264 was stalled alongside a consolidated, or a mogul skyscraper, she looked like an ancient beer glass set next an imported stein.

With the 264, when the 800 or the 1100 class were concerned, it was simply a case of keep out of our way or get smashed, Maje Sampson or no Maje Sampson, money question or no money question. Benevolent benefits fraternally proposed or ante-room signals confidentially put forth by the bald-headed 264 were of no sort of consequence with the modern giants that pulled a thousand tons in a string up a two-thousand-foot grade at better than twenty miles an hour. It was a clear yet cold, " You old tub, get out of our way, will you ? "

And the fast runners, like Moore and Hawksworth and Mullen and the Crowleys, Tim and Syme, had about as much consideration for Maje and his financial theories as their machines had for his machine. His jim-crow freight outfit did n't cut much of a figure in *their* track schedules.

So the Maje Sampson combination, but quite as brassy as though it had rights of the first class, dodged the big fellows up and down the line pretty successfully until the government began pushing troops into the Philippines, and there came days when a Rocky Mountain sheep could hardly have kept out of the way of the extras that tore, hissing and booming, over the mountains for 'Frisco. For a time the traffic came hot; so hot we were pressed to handle it. There was a good bit of skirmishing on the part of the passenger department to get the business, and then tremendous skirmishing in the operating department to deliver the goods. Every broken-down coach in the backyards was scrubbed up for the soldier trains. We aimed to kill just as few as possible of the boys en route to

the islands, though that may have been a mistaken
mercy. However, we handled them well; not a
man in khaki got away from us in a wreck, and in
the height of the push we put more live stock into
South Omaha, car for car, than has ever gone in
before or since.

It was November, and great weather for running,
and when the rails were not springing under the soldiers westbound, they were humming under the
steers eastbound. Maje Sampson, with his beer
kegs and his crackers and his 264 and his be-
knighted fireman, hugged the sidings pretty close
that week. Some of the trains had part of the
rights and others had the remainder. The 264 and
her train took what was left, which threw Maje
Sampson most of the time on the worn-out, run-
down, scrap rails that made corduroy roads of the
passing tracks. Then came the night that Moulton, the Philippine commandant, went through on
his special. With his staff and his baggage and his
correspondents and that kind he took one whole

train.   Syme Crowley pulled them, with Ben Sherer, conductor, and whatever else may be said of that pair, they deliver their trains on time.   Maje Sampson left Medicine Bend with Twenty-nine at noon on his regular run and tried to get west.   But between the soldiers behind him and the steers against him, he soon lost every visionary right he ever did possess. They laid him out nearly every mile of the way to the end of the run.   At Sugar Buttes they held him thirty minutes for the Moulton Special to pass, and, to crown his indignities, kept him there fifteen minutes more waiting for an eastbound sheep train. Sampson afterward claimed that Barnes Tracy, the despatcher that did it, was a Gold Democrat, but this never was proved.

It was nearing dark when the crew of local freight Twenty-nine heard the dull roar of the Moulton Special speeding through the cañon of the Rat.   A passenger train running through the cañon at night comes through with the far roll of a thousand drums, deepening into a rumble of thunder.   Then out and over all comes the threatening purr of the straining engine breaking into a storm of exhausts, until like a rocket the headlight bursts streaming from the black walls, and Moore on the 811, or Mullen with the 818, or Hawksworth in the 1110, tear with a fury of alkali and a sweep of noise over the Butte switch, past caboose and flats and boxes and the 264 like fading light. Just a sweep of darkened glass and dead varnish, a whirl of smoking trucks beating madly at the fishplates, and the fast train is up, and out, and gone !

Twenty-nine, local, was used to all this. Used to the vanishing tail lights, the measured sinking of the sullen dust, the silence brooding again over the desert with, this night, fifteen minutes more to wait for the east-bound stock train before they dared open the switch. Maje Sampson killed the time by going back to the caboose to talk equities with the conductor. It was no trick for him to put away fifteen minutes discussing the rights of man with himself; and with an angel of a fireman to watch the cab, why not ? The 264 standing on the siding was chewing her cud as sweet as an old cow, with maybe a hundred and forty pounds of steam to the right of the dial, maybe a hundred and fifty — I say maybe, because no one but Delaroo ever knew — when the sheep train whistled.

Sheep — nothing but sheep.   Car after car after car, rattling down from the Short line behind two spanking big engines.   They whistled, hoarse as pirates, for the Butte siding, and, rising the hill a mile west of it, bore down the grade throwing Dannah coal from both stacks like hydraulic gravel.

No one knew or ever will know how it happened. They cat-hauled men on the carpet a week about that switch.   The crew of the Moulton Special testified; the crews of the stock train testified; Maje Sampson testified; his conductor and both brakemen testified; the roadmaster and the section boss each testified, and their men testified — but however or whatever it was — whether the Moulton Special fractured the tongue, or whether the pony of the lead engine flew the guard, or whether the switch had been opened, or whether, in closing, the slip rail had somehow failed to follow the rod —

the double-headed stocker went into that Butte switch, into that Butte siding, into the peaceable old 264 and the Twenty-nine, local, like a lyddite shell, crashing, rearing, ripping, scattering two whole trains into blood and scrap. Destruction, madness, throes, death, silence; then a pyre of dirty smoke, a wail of sickening bleats, and a scream of hissing steam over a thousand sheep caught in the sudden shambles.

There was frightened crawling out of the shattered cabooses, a hurrying up of the stunned crews, and a bewildering count of heads. Both engine crews of the stock train had jumped as their train split the switch. The train crews were badly shaken; the head brakeman of the sheep train lay torn in the barbed-wire fencing the right of way; but only one man was missing — the fireman of Twenty-nine — Delaroo.

"Second 86 jumped west switch passing track and went into train 29, engine 264. Bad spill. Delaroo, fireman the 264, missing," wired Sugar Buttes to Medicine Bend a few minutes later.

Neighbor got up there by ten o'clock with both roadmasters and the wrecking outfit. It was dark as a cañon on the desert that night. Benedict Morgan's men tore splintered car timber from the débris, and on the knolls back of the siding lighted heaping bonfires that threw a light all night on the dread pile smoking on the desert. They dug by the flame of the fires at the ghastly heap till midnight; then the moon rose, an extra crew arrived from the Bend, and they got the derrick at work. Yet with all the toil when day broke the confusion looked worse confounded. The main line was so hopelessly blocked that at daylight a special with ties and steel was run in to lay a temporary track around the wreck.

"What do I think of it?" muttered Neighbor, when the local operator asked him for a report for Callahan. "I think there's two engines for the scrap in sight — and the 264, if we can ever find anything of her — and about a million sheep to pay for — " Neighbor paused to give an order and survey the frightful scene.

"And Delaroo," repeated the operator. "He wants to know about Delaroo — "

"Missing."

At dawn hot coffee was passed among the wreckers, and shortly after sunrise the McCloud gang arrived with the second derrick. Then the men of the night took hold with a new grip to get into the heart of the pile; to find — if he was there — Delaroo.

None of the McCloud gang knew the man they were hunting for, but the men from the Bend were soon telling them about Maje Sampson's Indian. Not a mute nod he ever gave; not a piece of tobacco he ever passed; not a brief word he ever spoke to one of the battered old hulks who rode and cut and slashed and stormed and drank and cursed with Benedict Morgan, was forgotten then. Every slewed, twisted, weather-beaten, crippled-up, gin-shivered old wreck of a wrecker — they were hard men — had something to say about Delaroo. And with their hair matted and their faces streaked and their shirts daubed and their elbows in blood, they said it — whatever it was, much or little — of Delaroo.

The picks swung, the derricks creaked, and all day with the heaving and the calling they toiled; but the sun was sinking before they got to the middle of it. Then Benedict Morgan, crawling under the drivers of the hind mogul, partly uncovered, edged out with a set face; he swore he heard breathing. It was alcohol to the veins of the double gang. Neighbor himself went in and heard — and stayed to fasten a grapple to pull the engine truck off the roof of a box car that was jammed over and against the mogul stack.

The big derrick groaned as the slack drew and the truck crashed through a tier of stays and swung whirling into the clear. A giant wrecker dodged the suspended wheels and raising his axe bit a hole into the jammed roof. Through that they passed a second grapple, and presently it gave sullenly, toppled back with a crash, and the foremost axman, peering into the opening, saw the heart of the wreck. Bending forward, he picked

up something struggling in his arms. They thought
it was a man; but it was a sheep, alive and unin-
jured, under all the horror: that was the breathing
they heard. Benedict Morgan threw the man and
his burden aside and stepped himself into the gap
and through. One started to follow, but the chief
of the wreckers waved him back. Close by where
the sheep had been freed stood Delaroo. He stood
as if with ear alert, so closely did the counterfeit
seem the real. So sure was the impression of life
that not until Morgan, speaking to the fireman, put
his hand on his shoulder did he realize that the
Indian stood quite dead just where the shock had
caught him in his cab.

Stumbling over the wreckage, they passed him
in the silence of the sunset from hand to hand
into the open. A big fellow, pallid and scared,
tottered after them, and when they laid the dead
man down, half fell at his side: it was Maje
Sampson.

It surprised everybody the way Maje Sampson
went to pieces after Delaroo was killed. The

Indian was carried back to the Bend and up to Sampson's and laid out in the God-forsaken parlor; but Maje was n't any good fixing things up that time. He usually shone on like occasions. He was the comforter of the afflicted to an extraordinary degree; he gave the usual mourner no chance to let up. But now his day was as one that is darkened. When Neighbor went up next night to see about some minor matters connected with the funeral and the precedence of the various dozen orders that were to march, he found Maje Sampson and Martie alone in the darkness of the parlor with the silent Delaroo.

Maje turned to the master mechanic from where Delaroo lay. " Neighbor, you might as well know it now as ary time. Don't you say so, Martie? Martie, what do you say? " Martie burst into tears; but through them Neighbor caught the engineer's broken confession. " Neighbor — I'm color blind." The master mechanic sat stunned.

" True as God's word. You might as well know it now. There's the man that stood between me and the loss of my job. It's been coming on me for two year. He knew it, that's why he stayed in my cab. He stayed because I was color blind. He knowed I'd git ketched the minute a new fireman come in, Neighbor. He watched the signals — Delaroo. I'm color blind, God help me." Maje Sampson sat down by the coffin. Martie hushed her crying; the three sat in the darkness.

"It wouldn't worry me so much if it wasn't f'r the family, Neighbor. The woman — and the boys. I ain't much a-savin'; you know that. If you can gi' me a job I can get bread an' butter out of, give it to me. I can't pull a train; my eyes went out with this man here. I wish to God it was me, and him standing over. A man that's color blind, and don't know a thing on God's earth but runnin' an engine, is worse 'n' a dead man."

Neighbor went home thinking.

They buried Delaroo. But even then they were not through with him. Delaroo had insurance in every order in the Bend, which meant almost every one on earth. There was no end to his benefit certificates, and no known beneficiaries. But when they overhauled his trunk they found every last certificate filed away up to the last paid assessment and the last quarter's dues. Then came a shock. People found out there was a beneficiary. While the fraters were busy making their passes Delaroo had quietly been directing the right honorable recording secretaries to make the benefits run to Neighbor, and so every dollar of his insurance ran. Nobody was more thunderstruck at the discovery than the master mechanic himself.

Yet Delaroo meant something by it. After Neighbor had studied over it nights the best of a month; after Maje Sampson had tried to take the color test and failed, as he persistently said he would; after he had gone to tinkering in the round-house, and from tinkering respectably, and by degrees down the hill to wiping at a dollar and forty cents a day with time and a half for overtime — Neighbor bethought himself all of a sudden one day of a paper Delaroo had once given him and asked him to keep.

He had put it away in the storekeeper's safe with his own papers and the drawings of his extension front end patent — and safely forgotten all about it. It was the day they had to go into the county court about the will that was not, when he recollected Delaroo's paper and pulled it out of its envelope. There was only a half sheet of paper, inside, with this writing from Delaroo to Neighbor:

R. B. A. — What is coming to me on ensurance give to Marty Sampson, wife of Maje.   Give my trunk to P. McGraw.

Rispk.,   P. De la roux.

When the master mechanic read that before the probate judge, Maje Sampson took a-trembling: Martie hid her face in her shawl, crying again. Maybe a glimmer of what it meant came for the first time in her life over her.   Maybe she remembered Delaroo as he used to sit with them under the kerosene lamp while Maje untiringly pounded the money question into him — smoking as he listened, and Martie mended on never-ending trousers.

Looking from Maje Sampson, heated with mono-
logue, to his wife, patiently stitching. No comments,
just looking as Pierre Delaroux could look.

Strange, Neighbor thought it, and yet, maybe,
not so strange. It was all there in the paper —
the torn, worn little book of Delaroo's life. She
was the only woman on earth that had ever done
him a kindness.

Nobody at Medicine Bend quite understood it;
but nobody at Medicine Bend quite suspected that
under all the barrenness up at Maje Sampson's an
ambition could have survived; yet one had. Martie
had an ambition. Way down under her faded
eyes and her faded dress there was an ambition,
and that for the least promising subjects in the
Rocky Mountains — the brickbats. Under the
unending mending and the poverty and the toil,
Martie, who never put her nose out of doors, who
never attended a church social, never ventured
even to a free public school show — had an ambition for the boys. She wanted the two biggest to
go to the State University; wanted them to go and

get an education. And they went; and Maje
Sampson says them boys, ary one, has forgotten
more about the money question than he ever knew.
It looks as if after all the brickbats might come
out; a bit of money in Martie's hands goes so far.

There are a few soldiers buried at the Bend.
Decoration Day there is an attempt at a turn-out;
a little speeching and a little marching. A thin,
straggle column of the same warped, bent old
fellows in the same faded old blue. Up the hill
they go and around to the cemetery to decorate.

When they turn at Maje Sampson's place —
there's a gate there now — Martie and more or
less of the boys, and Maje, kind of join in along
and go over with them carrying a basket or so of
flowers and a bucket of water.

The boys soon stray over to where the crowd
is, around the graves of the Heroes. But Martie
gets down by a grave somewhat apart and prods
the drifting gravel all up loose with an old case-
knife. You would think she might be kneading
bread there, the way she sways under her sun-

bonnet and gloves — for her little boiled hands are in gloves now.

"I don't know how much good it does Delaroo spiking up his grave once a year," Neighbor always winds up. "It may not do him a blamed bit of good, I don't say it does. But I can see them. I see them from the roundhouse; it does me good. Hm?"

"Maje?" he will add. "Why, I've got him over there at the house, wiping. I'm going to put him running the stationary if old John Boxer ever dies. When will he die? Blamed if I know. John is a pretty good man yet. I can't kill him, can I? Well, then, what's a matter with you?

"No, Maje don't talk as much as he used to; forgetting his passes more or less, too. Getting old like some more of us. He's kind of quit the money question; claims he don't understand it now as well as the boys do. But he can talk about Delaroo; he understands Delaroo pretty well — now."

Held for Orders

The Operator's Story

DE MOLAY FOUR

The Operator's Story

❧

DE MOLAY FOUR

VERY able men have given their lives to the study of Monsoon's headlight; yet science, after no end of investigation, stands in its presence baffled.

The source of its illumination is believed to be understood. I say believed, because in a day when yesterday's beliefs are to-morrow's delusions I commit myself personally to no theory. Whether it is a thing living or dead; whether malign to mackerel or potent in its influence on imperfectly understood atmospheric phenomena, I do not know. I doubt whether anybody knows, except maybe Monsoon himself. I know only that on the West End, Monsoon's headlight, from every point of view, stands high, and that on one occasion it stood between Abe Monsoon and a frightful catastrophe.

There have been of late studied efforts to introduce electric headlights on the Mountain Division. But there are grizzled men in the cab who look with distrust — silent, it is true, yet distrust — on the claims put forth for them. While Monsoon's headlight does its work — as it has done even long before Monsoon followed it to the West End, and will do long after he leaves the West End — why, they say, and reasonably enough, take on new and theoretical substitutes ?

While the discussion deepens and even rages in the Wickiup, Monsoon himself is silent. Brave men are modest men. Among ourselves we don't use adjectives ; where Monsoon is known it is not necessary to put anything ahead of his name — except, may be, once a month on the payroll when the cross-eyed accountant adds A. or Abe or Abraham, just as he happens to be fixed for time. Mon-

soon's name in itself stands for a great deal.   When
his brother engineers, men who have grown seamy
and weatherbeaten in the service, put up their
voices for Monsoon's headlight; or when talka-
tive storekeepers, who servilely jump at headquarters' experiments in order to court the favor of
the high, speak for electricity, Abe Monsoon himself is silent.   His light is there; let them take it
or leave it as they will.   If the Superintendent of
Motive Power should attempt to throw it out for
the new-fangled arrangement, Monsoon would
doubtless feel that it was not the first time Omaha
had gone wrong — and, for that matter, that neither
he nor anybody else had assurance it would be the
last.   However —

The story opens on Bob Duffy.   Bob, right from
the start, was what I call a good-looker, and, being
the oldest boy, he had more of the swing anyway.
When Martin came along, his mother had n't got
over thinking about Bob.   Doubtless she thought,
too, of Martin; but he was kind of overshadowed.
Bob began by clerking in the post-office and de-

livering mail to all the pretty girls.   His sympathy
for the girls was so great that after a while he
began passing out letters to them whether they
were addressed to the girls or to somebody else.
This gradually weakened his influence with the
government.

Martin began work in the telegraph office; he
really learned the whole thing right there at the
Bend under Callahan.   Began, carrying Western
Unions stuck at his waist under a heavy leather
belt.   He wore in those days, when he had real
responsibility, a formidable brown Stetson that appeared bent on swallowing his ears : it was about
the time he was rising trousers and eleven.   Nobody but Sinkers ever beat Martin Duffy deliver-
ing messages, and nobody, bar none — Bullhead,
McTerza, anybody — ever beat him eating pie.
It was by eating pie that he was able to wear the
belt so long — and you may take that either way.
But I speak gladly of the pie, because in the usual
course of events there is n't much pie in a despatcher's life.   There is, by very large odds,

more anxiety than pie, and I introduce the pie,
not to give weight to the incidents that follow
but rather to lighten them; though as Duffy has
more recently admitted this was not always the
effect of the pie itself.

I do not believe that Martin Duffy ever had an
enemy.   A right tight little chap he was, with
always a good word, even under no end of pressure
on the single track.   There's many a struggling
trainman that will look quick and grateful when
any fellow far or near speaks a word about Martin
Duffy.   Fast as he climbed, his head never
swelled.   His hats rested, even after he got a key,
same as the original Stetson, right on the wings of
his ears.   But his heart grew right along after his
head stopped, and that's where he laid over some
other railroad men I could mention if I had to,
which I don't — not here.

About the time it looked as if Martin would
make a go of it on the road, the post-office in-
spectors were thinking Bob would make a go of
it over the road.   But he was such a kid of a

fellow that the postmaster convinced the detectives Bob's way of doing things was simple foolishness, which it probably was, and they merely swore
him out of the service.

It was then that Martin reached out a hand to
his elder brother. There were really just the two
brothers; and back of them — as there is, somewhere, back of every railroad man — a mother.
No father — not generally; just a mother. A
quiet, sombre little woman in a shawl and a bonnet
of no special shape or size — just a shawl and a
bonnet, that's all. Anyhow, the Duffy boys'
mother was that way, and there's a lot more
like her. I don't know what gets the fathers;
maybe, very often, the scrap. But there's almost
always, somewhere, a mother. So after Martin
began to make a record, to help his mother and
his brother both, he spoke for Bob. Callahan
did n't hesitate or jolly him as he used to do
with a good many. He thought the company
could n't have too many of the Duffy kind; so
he said, "Yes, sure." And Bob Duffy was put

at work — same thing exactly : carrying messages, reading hair-destroyers and blowing his salary on pie.

But pie acts queer. Sometimes it makes a man's head solid and his heart big ; then again it makes a man's head big and his heart solid. I 'm not saying anything more now except that pie certainly acts different.

Bob Duffy was taller than Martin and I would repeat, handsomer ; but I can't, because Martin had absolutely no basis of beauty to start with. He was parchment-like and palish from sitting night after night and night after night over a sounder. Never sick a day in his life ; but always over the sounder until, sleeping or waking, resting or working, the current purred and purred through his great little head like a familiarity taking old tomcat. He could guess more off a wire than most men could catch after the whole thing had tumbled in.

So up and up ladder he went. Messenger, operator — up to assistant despatcher, up to a regular

trick despatcher.   Up to the orders and signing the
J. M. C., the letters that stood for our superintendent's name and honor.   Up to the trains and
their movements, up to the lives, then CHIEF! —
with the honor of the division all clutched in Martin
Duffy's three quick right fingers on the key and his
three quick left fingers on the pen at the same instant scratching orders across the clip.   Talk about
ambidexterity — Martin did n't know what it would
be like to use one hand at a time.   If Martin Duffy
said right, trains went right.   If he said wrong,
trains went wrong.   But Martin never said the
wrong; he said only the right.   Giddings knows;
he copied for him long enough.   Giddings and
plenty more of them can tell all about Martin
Duffy.

Bob did n't rise in the service quite so fast as
Martin.   He was rather for having a good time.
He did more of the social act, and that pleased his
mother, who, on account of her bonnet-and-shawl
complexion, did n't achieve much that way.   Martin, too, was proud of his brother, and as soon as

Bob could handle a wire, which was very soon
(for he learned things in no time) Martin got
Callahan to put him up at Grant as operator.
Bob got the place because he was Martin's
brother, nothing else. He held it about two
months, then he resigned and went to San 'Frisco.
He was a restless fellow ; it was Bob up and Bob
down. For a year he wandered around out there,
telegraphing, then he bobbed up again in Medicine
Bend out of a job. He wanted to go to work, and
— well, Callahan — Martin's brother, you know
— sent him up to Montair as night operator.
Three months he worked steady as a clock. Then
one night the despatchers at the Bend could n't get
Montair for two hours. It laid out Number Six
and a Special with the General Manager and made
no end of a row.

Martin said right off he ought to go. But there
was the little mother up home, silent, I expect, but
pleading-like. It was left largely to Martin, for
the young fellow was already chief; and that was
the trouble — he hated to bear down too hard ; so

he compromised by asking his superintendent not
to fire Bob but to set him back. They sent him
up as night man to Rat River, the meanest place
on the whole system. That was the summer of
the Templars' Conclave at San 'Frisco.

We worked the whole spring getting things up
along the line, from Omaha to the Sierras, for that
Conclave. Engines were overhauled, rolling stock
touched up, roadbed put in shape, everything shaken
from end to end. Not only were the passenger
records to be smashed, but beyond that a lot of our
big general officers were way-up Masons and meant
that our line should get not merely the cream of
the business but the cream of the advertising out
of the thing. The general tenor of the instruc-
tions was to nickel-plate everything, from the
catalpas to the target rods. For three months before the Conclave date we were busy getting ready
for it, and when the big day drew near on which
we were to undertake the moving and the feeding of
six thousand people one way on one track through
the mountains, the cartinks smoked cross-cut

and the Russian sectionmen began to oil their hair.

Callahan was superintendent under Bucks, then General Manager, and Martin Duffy, Chief Despatcher, Neighbor, Superintendent of Motive Power, and Doubleday, Division Master Mechanic, and with everything buttoned up on the West End we went that Sunday morning on the firing line to take the first of the Templar Specials.

Medicine Bend had the alkali pretty well washed out of its eyes, and never before in its history had it appeared really gay. The old Wickiup was decorated till it looked like a buck rigged for a ghost dance. Right after daybreak the trains began rolling in on Harold Davis's trick. Duffy had annulled all local freights and all through odds and evens, all stock tramps east and all westbound empties — everything that could be, had been suspended for that Sunday; and with it all there were still by five times more trains than ever before rolled through Medicine Bend in twenty-four hours.

It was like a festival day in the mountains. Even

the Indians and the squaw men turned out to see the fun. There was a crowd at the depot by five o'clock, when the first train rolled up the lower gorge with St. John's Commandery, Number Three from Buffalo; and the Pullmans were gay with bunting. The Medicine Bend crowd gave them an Indian yell and in two minutes the Knights, with their scalps in their hands as a token of surrender, were tumbling out of their sleepers into the crisp dawn. They were just like schoolboys, and when Shorty Lovelace — the local curiosity who had both feet and both hands frozen off the night he got drunk with Matt Cassidy at Goose River Junction — struck up on his mouth-organ " Put Me Off at Buffalo," they dropped seven dollars, odd, and three baggage checks into his hat while the crews were changing engines. It appeared to affect them uncommon, to see a fellow without any hands or feet play the mouth-organ and before sun-down Shorty made the killing of his life. With what he raked in that day he kept the city marshal guessing for three months — which was also pretty good for a man without any hands or feet.

All day it was that way : train after train and ovation after ovation.   The day was cool as a watermelon — August — and bright as a baby's face all through the mountains ; and the Templars went up into the high passes with all the swing and noise we could raise.   Harold Davis took it all morning steady from 4 A. M. at the despatcher's key.   He was used up long before noon ; but he stayed, and just at twelve o'clock, while a big Templar train from Baltimore was loading its commandery in front of the Wickiup after an early dinner, and a big Templar band played a tingling two-step, Martin Duffy stuck his dry, parchment face into the platform crowd, elbowed his way unnoticed through it, climbed the Wickiup stairs, walked into the despatcher's room, and, throwing off his hat and coat, leaned over Harold Davis's shoulder and took a transfer.

Young Giddings had been sitting there in a perspiration half an hour then ; he copied for Martin

Duffy that day. At noon they figured to get the last Templar over the Eagle Pass with the set of the sun. When Duffy took the key he never looked his force cleaner, only he was tired; Giddings could see that. The regular man had been sick a week and Martin had been filling in. Besides that, all Saturday, the day before, he had been spiking the line — figuring what could be annulled and what could n't; what could be run extra and what could be put into regulars. Callahan had just got married and was going out to the Coast on his wedding tour in Bucks's car. He had refused to look at an order after Saturday night. Sunday morning, and from Sunday morning on, it was all against Duffy. When the Chief took the middle trick there were fourteen Templar Specials still to come with the last one just pulling out of McCloud on the plains. They were ordered to run with right of track over all eastbound trains thirty minutes apart all the way through.

A minute after Martin Duffy sat in, the conductor of the train below registered out. There

was a yell pretty soon, and away went the Baltimore crowd — and they were corkers, too, those
Baltimore fellows, and travelled like lords.

At five o'clock in the evening the trains in the
West Division were moving just like clocks on
the hour and the half — thirty minutes, thirty minutes, thirty minutes — and, as far as young Giddings
could see, Duffy, after five booming hours, was
fresher than when he took the chair. The little
despatcher's capacity for work was something enor-
mous ; it was n't till after supper-time, with the
worst of the figuring behind him, and in the letting
down of the anxiety, that Martin began to look
older and his dry Indian hair began to crawl over
his forehead. By that time his eyes had lost their
snap, and when he motioned Giddings to the key,
and got up to walk up and down the hall in the
breeze, he looked like a wilted potato vine. His
last batch of orders was only a little one compared
with those that had gone before. But with the
changes to the different crews they read about like
this —

Telegraphic Train Order Number 68.   Mountain Division.

Superintendent's Office, August 8, 1892.

For Medicine Bend to C. and E. of Engines 664, 738, 810, 326, and 826.

Engines 664, 738, 810, and 326 will run as four Specials, Medicine Bend to Bear Dance.   Engine 826 will double-head Special 326 to summit of Eagle Pass.

First No. 80, Engine 179, will run two hours thirty minutes late Bear Dance to Medicine Bend.

Second No. 80, Engine 264, will run three hours and fifteen minutes late Bear Dance to Medicine Bend.

Third No. 80, Engine 210, will run four hours and thirty minutes late Bear Dance to Medicine Bend.

J. M. C.
D.

When young Giddings sat in, the sun was dropping between the Tetons.   In the yard the car-cleaners were polishing the plates on Bucks's private car and the darky cook was pulling chickens out of the refrigerator.   Duffy had thirteen Conclaves

moving smoothly on the middle trick.   The final
one was due, and the hostlers were steaming down
with the double-header to pull it over the Pass.
This, the last of the Commandery trains, was to
bring DE MOLAY COMMANDERY NUM-
BER FOUR of Pittsburg, and the orders were to
couple Bucks's car on to it for the run west.   De
Molay — and everybody had notice — was Bucks's
old commandery back in Pennsylvania, and he was
going to the end of the division that night with the
cronies of his youth.   Little fellows they were in
railroading when he rode the goat with them, but
now mostly, like him, big fellows.   Half a dozen
old salts had been pounding ahead at him all day
over the wire.   They were to join him and Mr.
and Mrs. Callahan for supper in the private car,
and the yellow cider lay on the thin-shaven ice and
the mountain grouse curled on the grill irons
when De Molay Four, Pittsburg, pulled into Medicine Bend.

We had seen a good many swell trains that day,
the swellest that ever pounded *our* fishplates, Pull-

mans solid, and the finest kind of people.   Boston, Washington, New York, Philadelphia sent some pretty gorgeous trains.   But with at least half the town on the platform, when De Molay Four rolled in it took their breath so they could n't yell till the Sir Knights began pouring from the vestibules and gave Medicine Bend their own lordly cheer.

Mahogany vestibules they were and extension platforms; salon lamps and nickeled handrails; buffet smoker and private diner: a royal train and a royal company; olive green from tender to tail lights — De Molay Four, Pittsburg.

Bucks's old gang spied him.   Modestly back under the portico, he stood near the ticket window, and they broke through at him solid.   They pulled him and hauled him and mauled him and passed him from hand to hand.   They stood him on his head and on his hands and on his feet again, and told him of something they wanted and wanted right off.

Bucks looked the least bit uncertain as he considered the opening request.   It was n't much in

some ways, what they asked; in other ways it was
a good deal.   He laughed and bantered and joked
them as long as they would stand it; then he
called up to Martin Duffy, who was leaning out
the despatchers' window, "We'll see how he
talks," laughed Bucks in his great big way.   "But,
boys, it's up to the Chief.   I'm not in it on the
orders, you know.   Martin," he called, as Duffy
bent his head, "they want fifteen minutes here to
stretch their legs.   Say they've been roasted in
the alkali all day.   Can you do anything for the
boys?"

The boys!   Big fellows in fezes, Shriner style,
and slim fellows in duck, sailor style, and bow-
legged fellows in cheviot, any old style.   Chaps in
white flannel, and chaps in gray, and chaps in blue.
Turkish whiskers and Key West cigars and Cru-
saders' togs — and, between them, Bucks, his head
most of the time in chancery.   It was the first
time they had seen him since he had made our
Jim Crow line into a system known from the
Boston and Maine to the Mexican Central, and,

bar none, run cleaner or better. The first time
they had seen him since he had made a name for
himself and for his road from Newport News to
'Frisco, and they meant now to kill him, dead.

You know about what it meant and about how
it went, how it had to go. What could Martin
say to the man who had made him all he was and
who stood, now a boy again among the boys of
his boyhood, and asked for fifteen minutes — a
quarter of an hour for De Molay Number Four?
It threw the little Chief completely off his schedules; just fifteen minutes was more than enough
to do that. All the work was done, the anxiety
nearly past — Martin had risen to rest his thumping head. But fifteen minutes; once in a lifetime
— Bucks asking it.

Duffy turned to big Jack Moore standing at his
side ready to pull De Molay over the Pass, and
spoke him low. Jack nodded; everything went
with Jack, even the turn-tables that stuck with
other engineers. Martin in his shirt-sleeves leaned
out the window and, looking down on the tur-

baned and turbulent mob, spoke so Bucks could hear.

"What is it?" demanded the most puissant commander of De Molay excitedly. "What does he say, Bucks?"

"What says the slave?" growled a second formidable crusader; "out with it!"

"All we want is fifteen minutes."

"You would n't turn us down on fifteen minutes this far from an oasis, would you, Bucks?" protested a glass-eyed Shriner.

Bucks looked around royally. "Fifteen minutes?" he drawled. "What's a quarter of an hour in a lifetime, Jackman, on the last oasis? Take off your clothes, you fellows, and take half an hour. Now will you be good?"

De Molay put up a Templar yell. They always get the good things of life, those Pittsburg men; things other fellows could n't begin to get. They passed the word through the sleepers, and the women began pouring from the vestibules. In two quick minutes out came the Duquesne band

in red pompons, duck trousers and military jackets,
white corded with black. The crowd broke, the
band marched down the platform and, striking up
the " Washington Post," opened ranks on the grass
plot above the Wickiup to receive the De Molay
guard. One hundred Knights Templar in fatigue
debouched into a bit of a park, and in the purple
of the sunset gave a commandery drill to the honor
of Bucks — Bucks and the West End.

It was Sunday night, and still as August could
make it. The battalion moving silent and mobile
as a streamer over the grass, marched, deployed
and rested. They broke, to the clear-cut music,
into crosses and squares and crescents and stars
until small boys went cross-eyed, and wheeling at
last on the line, they saluted Bucks — himself a
past grand commander — and the railroad men
yelled.

Meantime the General Manager's private car
had been pasted on the tail-end of De Molay Four,
and a pusher edging up, stuck its nose into the rear
vestibule. On the head end Jack Moore and

Oyster were backing down on the olive-green string with the two smoothest moguls on the division. Bucks and Neighbor had held back everything good all day for De Molay Four, down to engines and runners and conductor. Pat Francis carried the punch, and the little Chief sat again in the despatcher's chair for De Molay Four.

And while the lovely women strolled in the cool of the evening and the odor of mountain sweetness, and the guard drilled, and the band played, the Chief knit his brows over his train sheet. It looked now, re-arranged, re-ordered, readjusted and re-organized, as if a Gila Monster had crawled over it without wiping his feet. And when De Molay Four got ready to pull out, with Moore and Oyster on the throttles and old John Parker in the baggage, where he had absolutely nothing to do but drink cigars and smoke champagne and Pat Francis in the aisles, and Bucks, with Mr. and Mrs. Callahan and their crowd, in private Number Twelve — there was that much shouting and tooting and waving that Martin Duffy simply could n't think for a few seconds; yet he held them all, for life or for death, every last one, in the curve of his fingers.

So they stood ready in the gorge while Duffy studied wearily how to handle First, Second, and Third Eighty against them.

First, Second, and Third Eighty! If they could only have been wiped off the face of the rails as easy as they might have been wiped off a train sheet! But there they were, three sections, and big ones, of the California fast freight. High-class stuff for Chicago and New York that could n't be held or laid out that Sunday, not for a dozen Conclaves. All day First, Second, and Third Eighty had been feeling their way east through the mountains, trying to dodge the swell commanderies rolling by impudent as pay cars. But all the final plans to keep them out of every-body's way, out of the way of fez and turban and chapeau and Greek cross and crimson-splashed sleepers, were now dashed by thirty minutes at Medicine for De Molay Four.

Order after order went from under his hand.
New meeting-points for First, Second, and Third
Eighty and De Molay Four, otherwise Special 326.

Pat Francis snatched the tissues from Duffy's
hand and, after the battalion had dispersed among
their wives and sisters, and among the sisters
of the other fellow ; after the pomponed chaps
had chucked the trombones and cymbals and drums
at old John Parker's shins; after the last air-
cock had been tested and the last laggard crusader thrown forcibly aboard by the provost guard,
the double-header tooted, " Out! " and, with the
flutter of an ocean liner, De Molay Four pulled up
the gorge.

The orders buttoned in the reefers gave De Molay
a free sweep to Elcho, and Jack Moore and Oyster
were the men to take it, good and hard.   Moreover, there was glory aboard.   Pennsylvania nobs,
way-up railroad men, waiting to see what for motive power we had in the Woolly West ; how we
climbed mountains and skirted cañon walls, and
crawled down two and three per cent grades.   Then

with Bucks himself in the private car — what wonder they let her out and swung De Molay through
the gorge as maybe you 've seen a particularly
buoyant kite snake its tale out of the grass and
drag it careening skyward.   When they slowed
for Elcho at nightfall, past First and Second Eighty,
and Bucks named the mileage, the Pennsys refused
to believe it for the hour's run.   But fast as they
had sped along the iron trail, Martin Duffy's work
had sped ahead of them, and this order was waiting:

Telegraphic Train Order Number 79.
C. and E. Third No. 80, Rat River.
C. and E. Special 326, Elcho.
Third No. 80, Engine 210, and Special 326 will
meet at Rock Point.

J. M. C.
D.

With this meeting-point made, it would be
pretty much over in the despatchers' office.   Martin Duffy pushed his sallow hair back for the last
time, and, leaving young Giddings to get the last
O. K.'s and the last Complete on his trick, got
out of the chair.

It had been a tremendous day for Giddings, a tremendous day. Thirty-two Specials on the despatchers, and Giddings copying for the Chief. He sat down after Duffy, filled with a riotous importance because it was now, in effect, all up to Giddings, personally; at least until Barnes Tracy should presently kick him out of the seat of honor for the night trick. Mr. Giddings sat down and waited for the signature of the orders.

Very soon Pat Francis dropped off De Molay Four, slowing at Elcho, ran straight to the operator for his order, signed it and at once Order 79 was throbbing back to young Giddings at Medicine Bend. It was precisely 7.54 P. M. when Giddings gave back the Complete and at 7.55 Elcho reported Special 326, " out," all just like clockwork. What a head Martin Duffy has, thought young Giddings — and behold! all the complicated everlasting headwork of the trick and the day, and of the West End and its honor, was now up to the signature of Third Eighty at Rat River. Just Third Eighty's signature for the Rock Point meeting, and the biggest job ever tackled by a single-track road in America (Giddings thought) was done and well done.

So the ambitious Giddings by means of a pocket-mirror inspected a threatening pimple on the end of his chubby nose palming the glass skilfully so Barnes Tracy could n't see it even if he did interrupt his eruption, and waited for Bob Duffy, the Rat River nightman, to come back at him with Third Eighty's signature.   Under Giddings' eye, as he sat, ticked Martin Duffy's chronometer — the watch that split the seconds and chimed the quarters and stopped and started so impossibly and ran to a second a month — the watch that Bucks (who never did things by halves) had given little Martin Duffy with the order that made him Chief.   It lay at Giddings's fingers, and the minute hand wiped from the enamelled dial seven o'clock fifty-five, fifty-six, seven, eight — nine.   Young Giddings turned to his order book and inspected his entries like a methodical bookkeeper, and Martin Duffy's chronometer chimed the fourth quarter, eight o'clock.   One entry he had still to make. Book in hand he called Rat River.

" Get Third Eighty's signature to Order 79 and hurry them out," he tapped impatiently at Bob Duffy.

There was a wait. Giddings lighted his pipe the way Callahan always lighted *his* pipe — putting out his lips to catch all the perfume and blowing the first cloud away wearily, as Callahan always did wearily. Then he twirled the match meditatively, and listened, and got suddenly this from Bob Duffy at Rat River :

" I forgot Order 79," came Bob Duffy's message. " I let Third Eighty go without it. They left here at seven — fifty " —fifty something, Giddings never heard fifty what. The match went into the ink, the pipe into the water-pail, and Giddings, before Bob Duffy finished, like a drowning man was calling Elcho with the life and death, the Nineteen call.

" Hold Special 326 ! " he cried over the wire the instant Elcho replied.

But Elcho, steadily, answered this:

"Special — Three-twenty-six — left — here — seven-fifty-five."

Giddings, with both hands on the table, raised up like a drunken man. The West End was against it. Third Eighty in the open and going against the De Molay Four. Bucks, Callahan, wife — everybody — and Rock Point a blind siding that no word from anybody on earth could reach ahead of Third Eighty.

Giddings sprang to the open window and shouted to anybody and everybody to call Martin Duffy. But Martin Duffy spoke behind him.

"What do you want?" he asked; it came terribly quick on Giddings as he turned.

"What's the matter?" exclaimed Martin, looking into the boy's face. "Speak, can't you? What's the matter, Giddings?"

"Bob forgot Order 79 and let Third Eighty go without it — and Special 326 is out of Elcho," choked Giddings.

"*What?*"

"Bob at — Rat River — gave Third Eighty a clearance without the Order 79."

Martin Duffy sprang straight up in the air. Once he shut his lifted hands; once he looked at Giddings, staggering again through the frightful news, then he dropped into the chair, looked wildly around, seized his key like a hunted man, stared at his train sheet, grabbed the order book, and listened to Giddings cutting off one hope after another of stopping Special 326. His fingers set mechanically and he made the Rat River call; but Rat River was silent. With Barnes Tracy tiptoeing in behind on the instinct of trouble, and young Giddings shaking like a leaf, the Chief called Rat River. Then he called Elcho, asked for Special 326, and Elcho again repeated steadily:

"Special — 326 — left — here — on — Order — 79 — at — seven-fifty-five P.M."

Martin Duffy bent before the message; young Giddings, who had been whispering to Tracy, dropped on a stool and covered his face.

"Don't cry, Giddings." It was Duffy who

spoke; dry and parched his voice. " It's nothing you — could help." He looked around and saw Tracy at his elbow. " Barnes," he said, but he tried twice before his voice would carry. " Barnes — they will meet in the Cinnamon cut. Giddings told you? Bob forgot, forgot my order. Run, Giddings, for Benedict Morgan and Doubleday and Carhart — *quick !* "

Giddings ran, the Rat River call echoing again down the hall behind him. Rat River was closest to Rock Point — would get the first news of the wreck, and Martin Duffy was calling his recreant brother at the River; but the River was silent.

Doubleday and the company surgeon, Dr. Carhart, rushed into the room almost together. Then came with a storm the wrecking boss, Benedict Morgan; it was only an evil hour that brought Benedict Morgan into the despatchers' office. Stooped and silent, Martin Duffy, holding the chair, was calling Rat River. Carhart watched him just a moment, then he took Barnes Tracy aside and whispered — and, going back, bent over Duffy. The Chief pulled himself up.

"Let Tracy take the key," repeated the doctor. "Get away from the table a minute, Martin. It may not be as bad as you think."

Duffy, looking into the surgeon's face, put his hand on his arm. "It's the De Molay train, the Special 326, with Bucks's car, double-headed. Oh, my God — I can't stop them. Doctor, they will meet!"

Carhart unfastened the fingers on his arm. "Come away a minute. Let Tracy have the key," he urged.

"A head-ender, eh?" croaked Benedict Morgan from the counter, and with a frightful oath. "A head-ender!"

"Shut up, you brute!" hissed Carhart. Duffy's hands were creeping queerly up the sides of his head.

"Sure," growled Benedict Morgan, loweringly, "sure. Shut up. Of course. Shut up."

Carhart was a quick man. He started for the wrecker, but Duffy, springing, stopped him.

" For God's sake, keep cool, everybody," he exclaimed, piteously. There was no one else to talk,
to give the orders. Bucks and Callahan both on
the Special — maybe past order-giving now. Only
Martin Duffy to take the double load and the double
shame. He stared, dazed again, into the faces
around as he held to the fiery surgeon. " Morgan,"
he added steadily, looking at the surly wrecker,
" get up your crew, quick. Doubleday, make up
all the coaches in the yard for an ambulance train.
Get every doctor in town to go with you. Tracy,
clear the line."

The Master Mechanic and Benedict Morgan
clattered down stairs. Carhart, running to the
telephone, told Central to summon every medical
man in the Bend, and hurried out. Before he had
covered a block, roundhouse callers, like flaws of
wind before a storm, were scurrying the streets,
and from the tower of the fire-house sounded the
harsh clang of the emergency gong for the wreckers.

Caught where they could be caught, out of
saloons, beds, poker joints, Salvation barracks,

churches, — the men of the wrecking crew ran down the silent streets, waking now fast into life. Congregations were dispersed, hymns cut, prayers forgotten, bars deserted, hells emptied, barracks raided at that call, the emergency gong call, fell as a fire-bell, for the Mountain Division wrecking gang.

While the yard crews shot up and down the spurs switching coaches into the relief train, Benedict Morgan with solid volleys of oaths was organizing his men and filling them at the lunch counters with huge schooners of coffee. Carhart pushed again through the jam of men and up to the despatchers' office. Before and behind him crowded the local physicians with instrument bags and bandages. The ominous baggage deposited on the office floor, they sat down about the room or hovered around Carhart asking for details. Doubleday, tall and grim, came over from the roundhouse. Benedict Morgan stamped up from the yard — the Mountain Division was ready.

All three despatchers were in the room. John Mallers, the day man, stood near Tracy, who had

relieved Giddings. The line was clear for the
relief run. Elcho had been notified of the impending disaster, and at Tracy's elbow sat the Chief
looking fixedly at the key — taking the bob of
the sounder with his eye. A dozen men in the
room were talking; but they spoke as men who
speaking wait on the life of a fuse. Duffy, with
suspense deepening into frenzy, pushed Tracy's
hand from the key and, sliding into the chair,
began once more to call his brother at Rat River.

" R, T — R, T — R, T — R, T — " clicked the
River call. " R, T — R, T — R, T — Bob — Bob
— Bob," spelled the sender. " Answer me, an-
swer, answer. R, T — R, T — R, T — R, T — "

And Barnes Tracy edged away and leaned back
to where the shadow hid his face. And John
Mallers, turning from the pleading of the current,
stared gloomily out of the window across the yard
shimmering under the double relay of arc lights;
and young Giddings, who could n't stand it — just
could n't stand it — bending on his stool, shook
with gulping sobs.

The others knew nothing of the heartbreaking in the little clicks. But they all knew the track — knew where the trains would meet; knew they could not by any possibility see each other till they whirled together on the curve of the Cinnamon cut or on the trestle west of it and they waited only for the breaking of the suspense that settled heavily over them.

Ten, twenty, thirty, forty minutes went, with Martin Duffy at intervals vainly calling. Then — as the crack opens in the field of ice, as the snow breaks in the mountain slide, as the sea gives up at last its dead, the sounder spoke — Rat River made the despatcher's call. And Martin Duffy, staring at the copper coil, pushed himself up in his chair like a man that chokes, caught smothering at his neck, and slipped wriggling to the floor.

Carhart caught him up, but Duffy's eyes stared meaningless past him. Rat River was calling him, but Martin Duffy was past the taking. Like the man next at the gun, Barnes Tracy sprang into the chair with the I, I, D. The surgeon, Giddings helping, dragged Duffy to the lounge in Callahan's room — his Chief was more to Giddings then than the fate of Special 326. But soon confused voices began to ring from where men were crowding around the despatchers' table. They echoed in to where the doctors worked over the raving Chief. And young Giddings, helping, began, too, to hear strange things from the other room.

"The moon — "

"The *moon?*"

"The MOON!"

"*What?*"

Barnes Tracy was trying to make himself heard:

"The moon, damn it! MOON! That's English, ain't it? *Moon.*"

"Who's talking at Rat River?" demanded Benedict Morgan, hoarsely.

"Chick Neale, conductor of Third Eighty; their train is back at Rat River. God bless that man," stammered Barnes Tracy, wiping his forehead feverishly; "he's an old operator. He says Bob Duffy

is missing — tell Martin, quick, there is n't any
wreck — quick ! "

"What does Neale say ? " cried Doubleday with
an explosion.

Tracy thought he had told them, but he
had n't.   "He says his engineer, Abe Monsoon,
was scared by the moon rising just as they cleared
Kennel Butte," explained Tracy unsteadily.   "He
took it for the headlight of Special 326 and jumped
from his engine.   The fireman backed the train to
Rat River — see ? "

While Tracy talked, Mallers at the key was getting it all.   "Look here," he exclaimed, "did you
ever hear of such a mix-up in your life ?   The head
brakeman of the freight was in the cab, Neale says.
He and the engineer were talking about the last
Conclave train, wondering where they were going to
meet it, when the brakeman spied the moon coming
up around Kennel Butte curve.   'There's the 326
Special ! ' he yelled, and lighted out the gangway.
Monsoon reversed and jumped off after him so quick
he knocked the fireman over in the coal.   When

the fireman got up — he had n't heard a word of
it all — he could n't see anything ahead but the
moon. So he stops the train and backs up for the
two guys. When Neale and he picked them up
they ran right back to Rat River for orders. They
never got to Rock Point at all — why, they never
got two miles east of Rat River."

"And where 's Special 326 ?" cried Doubleday.

"At Rock Point, you loco. She must be there
and waiting yet for Third Eighty. The stopping
of the freight gave her plenty of time to make the
meeting-point, don't you see, and there she is —
sweating — yet. Neale is an old operator. By
Heaven ! Give me a man of the key against the
the world. Praise God from whom all blessings
flow !"

"Then there is n't to be any wreck ?" ventured a shy little lady homeopathic physician, who
had been crimped into the fray to help do up the
mangled Knights and was modestly waiting her
opportunity.

"Not to-night," announced Tracy with the

dignity of a man temporarily in charge of the entire division.

A yell went out of the room like a tidal wave. Doubleday and Benedict Morgan had not spoken to each other since the night of the roundhouse fire — that was two years.   They turned wonderstruck to each other.   Doubleday impulsively put out his hand and, before he could pull it in again, the wrecking boss grabbed it like a pay check. Carhart, who was catching the news from the rattle of young Giddings, went wild trying to repeat it to Duffy without losing it in his throat. The Chief was opening his eyes, trying to understand.

Medical men of violently differing schools, allopaths, homeopaths, osteopaths, eclectics — made their peace with a whoop.   A red-headed druggist, who had rung himself in for a free ride to the horror, threw his emergency packets into the middle of the floor.   The doctors caught the impulse: instrument cases were laid with solemn tenderness on the heap, and a dozen crazy men, joining hands around the pyred saws and gauze, struck up " Old Hundred."

Engineer Monsoon was a new man, who had been over the division only twice before in his life, both times in daylight. For that emergency Abe Monsoon was the man of all others, because it takes more than an ordinary moon to scare a thorough-bred West End engineer. But Monsoon and his moon headlight had between them saved De Molay Four from the scrap.

The relief arrangements and Monsoon's head-light were the fun of it, but there was more. Martin Duffy lay eleven weeks with brain fever before they could say moon again to him. Bob had skipped into the mountains in the very hour that he had disgraced himself. He has never shown up at Medicine since; but Martin is still Chief, and they think more of him on the Moun-tain district than ever.

Bucks got the whole thing when De Molay Four reached Rat River that night. Bucks and Calla-han and Moore and Oyster and Pat Francis got

it and smiled grimly.   Nobody else on Special 326
even dreamed of leaving a bone that Sunday
night in the Cinnamon cut.   All the rest of the
evening Bucks smiled just the same at the Knights
and the Knightesses, and they thought him for a
bachelor wonderfully entertaining.

A month later, when the old boys more or less
ragged came straggling back from 'Frisco, Bucks's
crowd stayed over a train, and he told his Pennsylvania cronies what they had slipped through in
that delay at Rock Point.

"Just luck," laughed one of the Eastern super-
intendents, who wore on his watch chain an enor-
mous Greek cross with "Our Trust is in God"
engraved on it.   "Just luck," he laughed, "was n't
it?"

"Maybe," murmured Bucks, looking through
the Wickiup window at the Teton peaks.   "That
is — you might call it that — back on the Penn.
Out here I guess they'd call it, Just God."

Dave Hawk.

Held for Orders

❧

The Trainmaster's Story

❧

OF THE OLD GUARD

The Trainmaster's Story

OF THE OLD GUARD

I NEVER found it very hard to get into trouble : as far back as I can remember that has come dead easy for me.

When this happened I had n't been railroading a month and I was up with my conductor on the carpet, sweating from sheer grogginess and excitement. The job of front-end brakeman on a mountain division is no great stake for a man ordinarily, but it was one for me, just then. We knew when we went into the superintendent's office that somebody was to get fired ; the only question was, who ? — the train crew or the operator ? Our engine crew were out of it ; it was up to the

conductor and to me.   Had the operator displayed
red signals ?   The conductor said, no ; I said, no ;
the operator said, yes : but he lied.   We could n't
prove it ; we could only put our word against his :
and what made it the worse for me, my conductor
was something of a liar himself.

I stood beading in a cold sweat for I could see
with half an eye it was going against us ; the
superintendent, an up-and-up railroad man every
inch and all business, but suspicious, was leaning
the operator's way the strongest kind.

There was n't another soul in the little room as
the three of us stood before the superintendent's
desk except a passenger conductor, who sat behind
me with his feet on the window ledge, looking out
into the yard.

" Morrison's record in this office is clean," the
superintendent was saying of the operator, who
was doing us smooth as smokeless powder, "he
has never to my knowledge lied in an investigation.   But, Allbers," continued the superintendent speaking bluntly to my conductor, " you 've

never told a straight story about that Rat River
switch matter yet.   This man is a new man," he
added, throwing a hard look at me.   " Ordinarily
I'd be inclined to take the word of two men
against one, but I don't know one at all and the
other has done me once.   I can't see anything for
it but to take Morrison's word and let you fellows
both out.   There was n't any wreck, but that's
not your fault ; not for a minute.''

" Mr. Rocksby," I protested, speaking up to
the division boss in a clean funk — the prospect of
losing my job that way, through a lying operator,
took the heart clean out of me — " you don't know
me, it is true, but I pledge you my word of
honor — "

" What's your word of honor ? " asked the
superintendent, cutting into me like a hatchet, " I
don't know any more about your word of honor
than I do about you."

What could I say ?   There were men who did
know me, but they were a long cry from the Rocky
Mountains and the headquarters of the Mountain

Division. I glanced about me from his face, gray as alkali, to Allbers, shuffling on the carpet, and to Morrison, as steady as a successful liar, taking my job and my reputation at one swallow ; and to the passenger conductor with the glossy black whiskers; but he was looking out the window. " What do I know about your word of honor ? " repeated Rocksby sharply. " Allbers, take your man and get your time."

A wave of helpless rage swept over me. The only thing I could think of, was strangling the lying operator in the hall. Then somebody spoke.

" Show your papers, you damn fool."

It came calm as sunshine and cold as a north-wester from the passenger conductor behind me, from Dave Hawk, and it pulled me into line like a bugle call. I felt my English all back at once. Everybody heard him and looked my way; again it was up to me. This time I was ready for the superintendent, or for that matter for the blooming Mountain Division. I had forgot all about my papers till Dave Hawk spoke. I put my hand, shaking, into my inside vest pocket for a piece of oilskin — it was all I had left; I was a good way from my base that year.   I laid the oilskin on the superintendent's table, unfolded it jealously and took out a medal and a letter, that in spite of the carefullest wrapping was creased and sweated. But the letter was from my captain and the bit of bronze was the Cross.   Rocksby picked up the letter and read it.

" Have you been in the British Army ? " he asked curtly.

" Yes, sir."

He scowled a minute over Picton's scrawl, laid it down and gratified his curiosity by picking up the medal.   He studied the face of the token, looked curiously at the dingy red ribbon, twirled it and saw the words on the reverse, " For Valour," and looked again at me.

" Where 'd you get this ? " he asked indicating the Victoria.

" In the Soudan, sir."

Dave Hawk kept right on looking out the window. Neither my conductor nor the operator seemed to know just what the row was. Nobody spoke.

"What' you doing here?" Rocksby went on.

"I came out to learn the cattle business." His brows went up easy-like. "They cleaned me out." Brows dropped gentle-like. "Then I went bad with mountain-fever," and he looked decent at me.

"You say you had your head out the cupola and saw the white signal?" he asked, sort of puzzled.

"I saw the white signal." Rocksby looked at the operator Morrison.

"We'll adjourn this thing," said he at last, "till I look into it a little further. For the present, go back to your runs."

We never heard any more of it. Allbers got out quick. I waited to pick up my stuff and turned to thank Dave Hawk; he was gone.

It was n't the first time Dave had pulled me out of the water. About two weeks before that I had crawled one night up on the front platform of the baggage at Peace River to steal a ride to Medicine

Bend on Number One. It was Dave's train. I
had been kicked out of the McCloud hospital two
days before without a cent, or a friend on earth
outside the old country, and I had n't a mind to
bother the folks at home any more, come Conan
or the devil.

The night was bitter bad, black as a Fuzzy and
sleeting out of the foothills like manslaughter.
When the train stopped at Rosebud for water,
what with gripping the icy hand-rail and trying
to keep my teeth steady on my knees I must have
been a hard sight.   Just as the train was ready to
pull out, Dave came by and poked his lantern full
in my face.

He was an older man than I, a good bit older,
for I was hardly more than a kid then, only spin-
dling tall, and so thin I could n't tell a stomach
ache from a back ache.   As I sat huddled down
on the lee step with my cap pulled over my head
and ears, he poked his light full into my face and
snapped, " Get out ! "

If it had been a headlight I could n't have been

worse scared, and I found afterward he carried the
brightest lamp on the division. I looked up into
his face and he looked into mine. I wonder if in
this life it is n't mostly in the face after all?
I could n't say anything, I was shaking in a chill
as I pulled myself together and climbed down into
the storm.

Yet I never saw a face harder in some ways than
Dave Hawk's. His visor hid his forehead and a
blackbeard covered his face till it left only his straight
cold nose and a dash of olive white under the eyes.
His whiskers loomed high as a Cossack's and his
eyes were onyx black with just such a glitter. He
knew it was no better than murder to put me off
in that storm at a mountain siding: I knew it;
but I did n't much care for I knew before very
long I should fall off, anyway. After I crawled
down he stood looking at me, and with nothing
better on I stood looking at him.

"If you get up there again I 'll break your
neck," he promised, holding up his lantern. I
was quiet; the nerve was out of me.

" Where you going ? " he asked shortly.

" Medicine Ben —— "

" Get into the smoker, you damn fool."

How it galvanized me. For twenty-four hours
I had n't eaten. I was just out of a hospital bed
and six weeks of mountain fever, but I braced at
his words like a Sioux buck. I hurried back ahead
of him to the smoking car, drenched wet, and
tough, I know. I looked so tough that the brakeman grabbed me the minute I opened the front door
and tried to kick me out. I turned snarling then,
crazy as a wolf all in a second, and somehow
backed the brakeman against the water cooler with
his windpipe twisted in my bony fingers like
a corkscrew. The train was moving out. I had
been cuffed and kicked till I would rather kill
somebody than not ; this seemed a fair chance for a
homicide. When the poor fellow's wind went
off — he was n't much of a scrapper, I fancy —
he whipped around in the aisle like a dying
rooster. As he struggled in my grip there behind him in the doorway stood Dave, lantern in

hand, looking on with a new face. This time he was smiling — Dave's smile meant just the parting of his lips over a row of glistening teeth; perfectly even teeth and under his black mustache whiter than ivory. It appeared to amuse him to see me killing the brakeman. The instant I saw Dave I let go and he watched the crestfallen trainman pull himself together.

"Guess you 'll let him alone now, won't you ? " said Dave pleasantly to my rattled assailant. "Sit down," he growled harshly at me, stringing his lantern on his arm. He walked unconcernedly down the aisle, and I dropped exhausted into the front seat facing the Baker heater. It was heavenly hot; red hot. I have loved a car heater ever since, and Baker to me, is hardly lower than the angels. My togs began to steam, my blood began to flow, the train boy gave me a wormy apple, an Irishman with a bottle of rank whiskey gave me a stinger and I wanted to live again. I curled up in the seat and in five minutes I was roasting, oh, such a heavenly roast; and dozing, Lord! what a heavenly doze, before that Baker heater. All night the forward truck beat and pounded under me: all night I woke and slept in the steaming, stinking air of the hot car. And whenever I opened my eyes I saw always the same thing, a topping tall conductor looming in the aisle, his green-hooded lamp, like a semaphore under his arm. And above, in the gloom, a bush of black beard and a pair of deep-set, shining eyes back under a peaked cap. Dave often comes back as I saw him, waking and dreaming, that night in the smoker of Number One.

It was breaking day when he bent over me.

"We're getting into the Bend," he said gruffly. "Got any money for breakfast?"

"I have n't a cent on God's earth." He put his hand in his pocket and pulling out a handful of loose bills shoved one into my fingers.

"I'll take it from you and gladly," I said sitting up. "But I'm not a beggar nor a tramp."

"Off track?"

"Yes. I'm going to enlist—" His teeth flashed. " That's worse than railroading, ain't it ? " Something came into my head like a rocket.

" If I could get started railroading ——"

" Get started easy enough."

That's how I happened to show him my Victoria. He gave me a card to the trainmaster, and next day I went to braking for Allbers, who, by the way, was the biggest liar I ever knew.

But the morning I got into Medicine Bend that first time on Number One I had another scare. I went into the lunch room for coffee and sandwiches and threw my bill at the boy. He opened it, looked at it and looked at me.

" Well," I growled, for I was impudent with luck and a hot stomach. "Good, ain't it ? "

" Smallest you got ? "

I nodded as if I had a pocket full. He hustled around and came back with a handful of money. I said nothing but when he spread it out before me I sat paralysed. I had just assumed that Dave had given me a dollar. Sinkers, deducting the price of two coffees and six sandwiches from the bill counted out nineteen dollars and thirty cents for me.

That change kept me running for a month, and after my first pay day I hunted up Dave to pay him back. I found him in the evening. He was sitting alone on the eating-house porch, his feet up against the rail, looking at the mountains in the sunset.

" Never mind," he said, as I held out a twenty dollar bill and tried to speak my little piece. He did not move except to wave back my hand.

" Oh, but I can't let you do that —— " I protested.

" Put up your money, Tommie." He called me Tommie.

" No," he repeated putting by my hand ; his face set hard, and when Dave's face did set it set stony. " Put up your money ; you don't owe me anything. I stole it."

It was a queer deal out on the West End in

those days.   It was a case of wide open from the
river to the Rockies.   Everybody on the line from
the directors to the car-tinks were giving the company the worst of it.   The section hands hooked
the ties for the maintenance, the painters drank the
alcohol for the shellac, the purchasing agent had
more fast horses than we had locomotives, and
what made it discouraging for the conductors, the
auditors stole what little money the boys did turn
in.

A hard place to begin railroading the old line
was then: but that's where I had to tackle the
game, and in all the hard crowd I mixed with
Dave Hawk was the only big man on the division.
There were others there who fixed the thing up
by comparing notes on their collections and turning in percentages to make their reports look right.
But Dave was not a conspirator; never made a
confidant of any man in his stealing or his spend-
ing, and despised their figuring.   He did as he
pleased and cared for no one; no superior had any
terror for Dave.   He had a wife somewhere back

east of the river, they said, that had sold him out —
that's why he was in the mountains — and he
lived among free and easy men a lonely life.   If
anybody ever got close to him, I think maybe I
did, though I was still only a freight conductor
when the lightning struck the division.

It came with a clean sweep through the general
offices at the River.   Everybody in the auditing
department, the executive heads down to general
manager and a whole raft of East End conductors.
It was a shake-out from top to bottom, and the
bloods on our division went white and sickly very
fast.

Of course it was somebody's gain.   When the
heads of our passenger conductors began to drop,
they began setting up freight men.   Rocksby had
resigned a year earlier, and Haverly, his successor,
an ex-despatcher and as big a knave as there was
on the pay roll, let the men out right and left
with the sole idea of saving his own scalp.   By
the time I was put up to a passenger train the old
force was pretty much cleared out except Dave.

Every day almost, we looked to see him go. Everybody loved him because he was a master railroad man, and everybody except Dave himself was apprehensive about his future. He moved on just the same, calm and cold as icewater, taking the same old chances, reckless of everything and everybody. I never knew till afterward, but the truth was Haverly with all his bluff talk was just enough afraid of Dave Hawk to want to let him alone. The matter, though, focused one day up in the old office in an unexpected way.

Haverly's own seat got so hot that bedeviled by his fears of losing it and afraid to discharge Dave, who now sailed up and down the line reckless as any pirate of the Spanish Main, he cowered, called Dave into the little room at the Wickiup and asked him to resign. In all the storm that raged on the division the old conductor alone had remained calm. Every day it was somebody's head off; every night a new alarm; Dave alone ignored it all. He was, through it all, the shining mark, the daredevil target; yet he bore a charmed

life and survived every last associate. Then
Haverly asked him to resign. Dave, bitter angry,
faced him with black words in his throat.

"It 's come to a showdown," muttered the
superintendent uneasily after a minute's talking.
"Do you want to resign?"

Dave eyed the mountains coldly.   "No."

"You 'll have to — "

"Have to?"   Hawk whirled dark as a storm.
"Have to?   Who says so?"

The superintendent shifted the paperweight on
the desk uncomfortably.

"Why should I resign?" demanded the old
conductor angrily.   "Resign?"   He rose from
his chair.   "You know I 'm a thief.   You 're
a thief yourself.   You helped make me one.   I 've
carried more men for you than for anybody else
on the whole division.   I don't resign for anybody.
Discharge me, damn you.   I don't ask any odds
of you."

Haverly met it sullenly, yet he did n't dare do
anything.   He knew Dave could ruin him any

day he chose to open his mouth. What he did not know was that Dave Hawk was molded in a class of men different from his own. Even dishonor was safe in the hands of Dave Hawk.

There was no change after, except that darker, moodier, lonelier than ever, Dave moved along on his runs, the last of the Old Guard. Better railroad man than he never took a train out of division. Stress of wind or stress of weather, storm, flood or blockade, Dave Hawk's trains came and went on time or very close. So he rode, grim old privateer, with his letters of marque on the company's strongbox, and Haverly trembled night and day till that day came that fear had foretold to him. A clap of thunder struck the Wickiup and Haverly's head fell low; and Dave Hawk sailed boldly on.

I was extra passenger man when John Stanley Bucks took the West End. He came from south of our country, and we heard great things about the new superintendent and about what would happen as soon as he got into the saddle. What few of the old men in the Wickiup were left looked at Bucks just once and began to arrange their temporal affairs. His appearance bore out his reputation. Only, everybody while pretty clear in his own mind as to what he would do — that is, as to what he would have to do — wondered what Dave would do.

He and Bucks met. I could n't for the life of me help thinking when they struck hands, this grizzled mountaineer and this contained, strong, soldierly executive who had come to command us, of another meeting, I once saw when I carried Crook out on a special and watched him at Bear Dance strike hands with the last of the big fighting chiefs of the mountain Sioux.

For three months Bucks sat his new saddle without a word or an act to show what he was thinking : then there came from the little room a general order that swept right and left from trainmaster to wrecking boss. The last one of the old timers in the operating department went except Dave Hawk.

The day the order was bulletined Bucks sent

for Dave; sent word by me he wanted to see him.

"Come on," said Dave to me when I gave him the message.

"What do you want me for?"

"Come on," he repeated, and, greatly against my inclination, I went up with him. I looked for a scene.

"Dave, you've been running here a good while, have n't you?" Bucks began.

"Long as anybody, I guess," said Dave curtly.

"How many years?"

"Nineteen."

"There's been some pretty lively shake-outs on the system lately," continued Bucks; the veteran conductor looked at him coldly. "I am trying to shape things here for an entire new deal."

"Don't let me stand in your way," returned Dave grimly.

"That's what I want to see you about."

"It need n't take long," blurted Dave.

"Then I'll tell you what I want ——"

"I don't resign. You can discharge me any minute."

"I would n't ask any man to resign, Dave, if I wanted to discharge him. Don't make a mistake like that. I suppose you will admit there's room for improvement in the running of this division?"

Dave never twitched. "A whole lot of improvement," Bucks, with perceptible emphasis, added. It came from the new superintendent as a sort of gauntlet and Dave picked it up.

"I guess that's right enough," he replied candidly, "there is room for a whole lot of improvement. If I sat where you do I'd fire every man that stood in the way of it, too."

"That's why I've sent for you," Bucks resumed.

"Then drop the chinook talk and give me my time."

"You don't understand me yet, Dave. I want you to give up your run. I want your friend, Burnes here, to take your run——"

A queer shadow went over Dave's face. When
Bucks began he was getting a thunderstorm on.
Somehow the way it ended, the way it was coming
about — putting me into his place — I, the only
boy on the division he cared " a damn " about —
it struck him, as it struck me, all in a heap. He
couldn't say a word; his eyes went out the window into the mountains: something in it looked
like fate. For my part I felt murder guilty.

" What I want you to do, Dave," added Bucks
evenly, " is to come into the office here with me
and look after the train crews. Just at present
I've got to lean considerably on a trainmaster, do
you want the job ? "

The silent conductor turned to stone.

" The men who own the road are new men,
Dave; they didn't steal it. They bought it and
paid for it. They want a new deal and they propose to give a new deal to the men. They will
pay salaries a man can live on honestly; they
will give no excuse for knocking down; they want
what's coming to them, and they propose the men

shall have their right share of it in the pay checks.

" But there 's more than that in it. They want to build up the operating force, as fast as it can be built, from the men in the ranks. I aim to make a start now on this division. If you 're with me, hang up your coat here the first of the month, and take the train crews."

Dave left the office groggy. The best Bucks could do he could n't get a positive answer out of him. He was overcome and could n't focus on the proposition. Bucks saw how he had gone to pieces and managed diplomatically to leave the matter open, Callahan, whom Bucks had brought with him as assistant, filling in meanwhile as trainmaster.

The matter was noised. It was known that Dave, admittedly the brainiest and most capable of the Old Guard had been singled out, regardless of his past record for promotion. " I 'm not here sitting in judgment on what was done last year," Bucks had said plainly. " It 's what is done this year and next that will count in this office." And

the conductors, thinking there was a chance, be-
lieving that at last if they did their work right they
would get their share of the promotions, began to
carry their lanterns as if they had more important
business than holding up stray fares.

Meantime Dave hung to his run. Somehow
the old run had grown a part of him and he
could n't give it up. When he told Bucks at the
end of the week that he would like another week
to make his decision the superintendent waved it
to him. Everybody began to make great things
of Dave : some of the boys called him trainmaster
and told him to drop his punch and give Tommie
a show.

He did n't take the humor the way one would
expect. Always silent he grew more than that;
sombre and dejected. We never saw a smile on
his face. " Dave is off," muttered Henry Cavanaugh, his old baggageman, " I don't understand it. He's off. You ought to talk to him,
Tommie. You're the only man on the division
can do it."

I was ordered west that night to bring a military special from Washakie. I rode up on Dave's train. The hind Los Angeles sleeper was loaded light, and when Dave had worked the train and walked into the stateroom to sort his collections, I followed him. We sat half an hour alone and undisturbed, but he would n't talk. It was a heavy train and the wind was high.

We made Rat River after midnight, and I was still sitting alone in the open stateroom when I saw Dave's green light coming down the darkened aisle. He walked in, put his lamp on the floor, sat down, and threw his feet on the cushions.

"How 's Tommie to-night?" he asked, leaning back as if he had n't seen me before, in his old teasing way. He played light heart sometimes; but it was no more than played: that was easy seeing.

"How 's Dave?" He turned, pulled the window shade and looked out. There was a moon and the night was bright, only windy.

"What are you going to do with Bucks, Dave?"

" Do you want my punch, Tommie ? "

" You know better than that, don't you ? "

" I guess so."

" You 're blue to-night.   What 's the matter ? "
He shifted and it was n't like him to shift.

" I 'm going to quit the West End."

" Quit ?   What do you mean ?   You 're not
going to throw over this trainmaster offer ? "

" I 'm going to quit."

" What 's the use," he went on slowly.   " How
can I take charge of conductors, talk to conductors ?   How can I discharge a conductor for stealing when he knows I 'm a thief myself ?   They
know it; Bucks knows it.   There 's no place
among men for a thief."

" Dave, you take it too hard ; everything ran
wide open here.   You 're the best railroad man
on this division ; everybody, old and new, admits
that."

" I ought to be a railroad man.   I held down a
division on the Pan Handle when I was thirty
years old."

"Were you a railroad superintendent at thirty?"

"I was a trainmaster at twenty-seven. I'm forty-nine now, and a thief. The woman that ditched me is dead: the man she ran away with is dead: my baby is dead, long ago." He was looking out, as he spoke, on the flying desert ashen in the moonlight. In the car the passengers were hard asleep and we heard only the slew of the straining flanges and the muffled beat of the heavy truck under us.

"There's no law on earth that will keep a man from leaving the track once in a while," I argued; "there's none to keep him from righting his trucks when the chance is offered. I say, a man's bound to do it. If you won't do it here, choose your place and I'll go with you. This is a big country, Dave. Hang it, I'll go anywhere. You are my partner, are n't you?"

He bent to pick up his lantern, "Tommie, you're a great boy."

"Well, I mean it." He looked at his watch, I pulled mine: it was one o'clock.

"Better go to sleep, Tommie." I looked up into his face as he rose. He looked for an instant steadily into mine. "Go to bed, Tommie," he smiled, pulling down his visor, and turning, he walked slowly forward. I threw myself on the couch and drew my cap over my eyes. The first thing I felt was a hand on my shoulder. Then I realized I had been asleep and that the train was standing still. A man was bending over me, lantern in hand. It was the porter.

"What's wrong?" I exclaimed.

"There's trouble up ahead, Mr. Burnes," he exclaimed huskily. I sprang to my feet. "Have you got your pistol?" he stuttered.

Somebody came running down the aisle and the porter dodged like a hare behind me. It was the hind-end brakeman, but he was so scared he could not speak. I hurried forward.

Through the head Los Angeles sleeper, the San Francisco cars and the Portland I ran without meeting a living soul; but the silence was ominous. When I caught a glimpse of the inside of the chair car, I saw the ferment. Women were screaming and praying, and men were burrowing under the foot-rests. "They've killed everybody in the smoker," shouted a travelling man, grabbing me.

"Damnation, make way, won't you!" I exclaimed, pushing away from him through the mob. At the forward door, taking me for one of the train robbers, there was another panic. Passengers from the smoker were jammed together there like sardines. I had to pile them bodily across the seats to get through and into the forward car.

It was over. The front lamps were out and the car smoking bluish. A cowboy hung pitched head and arms down over the heater seat. In the middle of the car Henry Cavanaugh, crouching in the aisle, held in his arms Dave Hawk. At the dark front end of the coach I saw the outline of a man sprawled on his face in the aisle. The news agent crawled out from under a seat. It must have been short and horribly sharp.

They had flagged the train east of Bear Dance.

Two men boarded the front platform of the smoker and one the rear. But the two in front opened the smoker door just as Dave was hurrying forward to investigate the stop. He was no man to ask questions. He saw the masks and covered them instantly. Dave Hawk any time and anywhere was a deadly shot. Without a word he opened on the forward robbers. A game cowboy back of him pulled a gun and cut into it; and was the first to go down, wounded. But the train boy said, Hawk himself had dropped the two head men almost immediately after the firing began and stood free handed when the man from the rear platform put a Winchester against his back. Even then, with a hole blown clean through him, he had whirled and fired again; we found the man's blood on the platform in the morning, but, whoever he was, he got to the horses and got away.

When I reached Dave, he lay in his baggageman's arms. We threw the carrion into the baggage car and carried the cowboy and the conductor back into the forward sleeper. I gave the go-ahead orders and hurried again to the side of the last of the Old Guard. Once his eyes opened, wandering stonily; but he never heard me, never knew me, never spoke. As his train went that morning into division he went with it. When we stopped, his face was cold. It was up to the Grand Master.

A game man always, he was never a cruel one. He called himself a thief. He never hesitated with the other men high and low to loot the company. The big looters were financiers: Dave was only a thief, yet gave his life for the very law he trampled under foot.

Thief, if you please; I don't know: we need n't quarrel about the word he branded himself with. Yet a trust of money, of friendship, of duty were safer far in Dave Hawk's hands than in the hands of abler financiers.

I hold him not up for a model, neither glory in his wickedness. When I was friendless, he was my friend: his story is told.

Jimmy the Wind.

Held for Orders

The Yellow Mail Story

JIMMIE THE WIND

The Yellow Mail Story

✳

JIMMIE THE WIND

THERE was n't another engineer on the division that dared talk to Doubleday the way Jimmie Bradshaw talked.

But Jimmie had a grievance, and every time he thought about it, it made him nervous.

Ninety-six years. It seemed a good while to wait ; yet in the regular course of events on the Mountain Division there appeared no earlier prospect of Jimmie's getting a passenger run.

" Got your rights, ain't you ? " said Doubleday, when Jimmie complained.

" I have and I have n't," grumbled Jimmie, winking hard ; " there 's younger men than I am on the fast runs."

" They got in on the strike; you 've been told that a hundred times. We can't get up another strike just to fix you out on a fast run. Hang on to your freight. There 's better men than you in Ireland up to their belt in the bog, Jimmie."

" It 's a pity they did n't leave you there, Doubleday."

" You 'd have been a good while hunting for a freight run if they had."

Then Jimmie would get mad and shake his finger and talk fast : " Just the same, I 'll have a fast run here when you 're dead."

" Maybe; but I 'll be alive a good while yet, my son," the master mechanic would laugh. Then Jimmie would walk off very warm, and when he got into the clear with himself, he would wink furiously and say friction things about Doubleday that need n't now be printed, because it is different. However, the talk always ended that way, and Jimmie Bradshaw knew it always would end that way.

The trouble was, no one on the division would

take Jimmie seriously, and he felt that the ambition
of his life would never be fulfilled; that he would
go plugging to gray hairs and the grave on an old
freight train; and that even when he got to the
right side of the Jordan there would still be something like half a century between him and a fast
run.   It was funny to hear him complaining about
it, for everything, even his troubles, came funny to
him, and in talking he had an odd way of stutter-
ing with his eyes, which were red.   In fact, Jimmie was nearly all red; hair, face, hands — they
said his teeth were sandy.

When the first rumors about the proposed Yellow Mail reached the mountains Jimmie was running a new ten-wheeler; breaking her in on a
freight " for some fellow without a lick o' sense to
use on a limited passenger run," as Jimmie ob-
served bitterly.   The rumors about the mail came
at first like stray mallards, opening signs of winter,
and as the season advanced flew thicker and faster.
Washington never was very progressive in the
matter of improving the transcontinental service,

but once by mistake they put in a postmaster-
general down there, who would n't take the old
song. When the bureau fellows that put their
brains up in curl papers told him it could n't be done
he smiled softly, and sent for the managers of the
crack lines across the continent, without suspecting
how it bore incidentally on Jimmie Bradshaw's
grievance against his master mechanic.

The postmaster-general called the managers of
the big lines, and they had a dinner at Chamberlain's, and *they* told him the same thing. " It has
been tried," they said in the old, tired way ; " really
it can't be done."

" California has been getting the worst of it for
years on the mail service," persisted the postmaster-
general moderately. " But Californians ought to
have the best of it. We don't think anything
about putting New York mail in Chicago in twenty
hours. It ought to be simple to cut half a day
across the continent and give San Francisco her
mail a day earlier. Where's the fall down ? " he
asked, like one refusing no for an answer.

The general managers looked at our representative sympathetically, and coughed cigar smoke his way to hide him.

" West of the Missouri," murmured a Pennsylvania swell, who pulled indifferently at a fifty-cent cigar. Everybody at the table took a drink on the *exposé*, except the general manager who sat at that time for the Rocky Mountains.

The West End representative was unhappily accustomed to facing the finger of scorn on such occasions. It had become with our managers a tradition. There was never a conference of transcontinental lines in which we were not scoffed at as the weak link in the chain of everything — mail, passenger, specials, what not — the trouble was invariably laid at our door.

This time a new man was sitting for the line at the Chamberlain dinner; a youngish man with a face that set like cement when the West End was trod on.

The postmaster-general was inclined, from the reputation we had, to look on our man as one

looks at a dog without a pedigree, or at a dray
horse in a bunch of standard-breds. But something in the mouth of the West End man gave him
pause; since the Rough Riders, it has been a bit
different with verdicts on things Western. The
postmaster-general suppressed a rising sarcasm with
a sip of Chartreuse, for the dinner was ripening,
and waited; nor did he mistake, the West Ender
was about to speak.

"Why west of the Missouri?" he asked, with
a lift of the face not altogether candid. The Pennsylvania man shrugged his brows; to explain might
have seemed indelicate.

"If it is put through, how much of it do you
propose to take yourself?" inquired our man,
looking evenly at the Allegheny official.

"Sixty-five miles, including stops from the New
York post-office to Canal Street," replied the Pennsylvania man, and his words flowed with irritating
ease.

"What do you take?" continued the man
with the jaw, turning to the Burlington repre-

sentative, who was struggling, belated, with an artichoke.

" *About* seventy from Canal to Tenth and Mason. Say, seventy," repeated the " Q " manager, with the lordliness of a man who has miles to throw at almost anybody, and knows it.

" Then suppose we say sixty-five from Tenth and Mason to Ogden," suggested the West Ender. There was a well-bred stare the table round, a lifting of glasses to mask expressions that might give pain. Sixty-five miles an *hour ?* Through the *Rockies ?*

The postmaster-general struck the table quick and heavily ; he did n't want to let it get away. " Why, hang it, Mr. Bucks," he exclaimed with emphasis, " if you will say sixty, the business is done. We don't ask you to do the Rockies in the time these fellows take to cut the Alleghenies. Do sixty, and I will put mail in 'Frisco a day earlier every week in the year."

" Nothing on the West End to keep you from doing it," said General Manager Bucks. He

had been put up then only about six months.
" But —— "

Every one looked at the young manager. The
Pennsylvania man looked with confidence, for he
instantly suspected there must be a string to such
a proposition, or that the new representative was
" talking through his hat."

" But what ? " asked the Cabinet member,
uncomfortably apprehensive.

" We are not putting on a sixty-five mile schedule just because we love our country, you understand, nor to heighten an already glorious reputation.
Oh, no," smiled Bucks faintly, " we are doing it
for ' the stuff.' You put up the money ; we put
up the speed. Not sixty miles ; sixty-five — from
the Missouri to the Sierras. No ; no more wine.
Yes, I will take a cigar."

The trade was on from that minute. Bucks
said no more then ; he was a good listener. But
next day, when it came to talking money, he talked
more money into the West End treasury for one
year's running than was ever talked before on a

mail contract for the best three years' work we
ever did.

When they asked him how much time he wanted
to get ready, and told him to take plenty, three
months was stipulated. The contracts were drawn,
and they were signed by our people without hesitation because they knew Bucks. But while the
preparations for the fast schedule were being made,
the government weakened on signing. Nothing
ever got through a Washington department without hitch, and they said our road had so often failed
on like propositions that they wanted a test. There
was a deal of wrangling, then a test run was agreed
on by all the roads concerned. If it proved suc-
cessful, if the mail was put to the Golden Gate on
the second of the schedule, public opinion and the
interests in the Philippines, it was concluded, would
justify the heavy premium asked for the service.

In this way the dickering and the figuring became, in a measure, public, and keyed up everybody
interested to a high pitch. We said nothing for
publication, but under Bucks's energy sawed wood

for three whole months. Indeed, three months goes as a day getting a system into shape for an extraordinary schedule. Success meant with us prestige; but failure meant obloquy for the road and for our division chief who had been so lately called to handle it.

The real strain, it was clear, would come on his old, the Mountain, division; and to carry out the point, rested on the Motive Power of the Mountain Division; hence, concretely, on Doubleday, master mechanic of the hill country.

In thirty days, Neighbor, superintendent of the Motive Power, called for reports from the division master mechanics on the preparations for the Yellow Mail run, and they reported progress. In sixty days he called again. The subordinates reported well except Doubleday. Doubleday said merely, " Not ready "; he was busy tinkering with his engines. There was a third call in eighty days, and on the eighty-fifth a peremptory call. Everybody said ready except Doubleday. When Neighbor remonstrated sharply he would say only that he would be ready in time. That was the most he would promise, though it was generally understood that if he failed to deliver the goods he would have to make way for somebody that could.

The Plains Division of the system was marked up for seventy miles an hour, and, if the truth were told, a little better ; but, with all the help they could give us, it still left sixty for the mountains to take care of, and the Yellow Mail proposition was conceded to be the toughest affair the Motive Power at Medicine Bend had ever faced. However, forty-eight hours before the mail left the New York post-office Doubleday wired to Neighbor, " Ready " ; Neighbor to Bucks, " Ready " ; and Bucks to Washington, " Ready " — and we were ready from end to end.

Then the orders began to shoot through the mountains. The test run was of especial importance, because the signing of the contract was believed to depend on the success of it. Once signed, accidents and delays might be explained ; for the test run there must be no delays. Despatchers were

given the eleven, which meant Bucks; no lay-outs,
no slows for the Yellow Mail.   Roadmasters were
notified; no track work in front of the Yellow
Mail.   Bridge gangs were warned, yard masters
instructed, section bosses cautioned, track walkers
spurred — the system was polished like a barkeep-
er's diamond, and swept like a parlor car for the
test flight of the Yellow Mail.

Doubleday, working like a boiler washer, spent
all day Thursday and all Thursday night in the
roundhouse.   He had personally gone over the engines that were to take the racket in the mountains.
Ten-wheelers they were, the 1012 and the 1014,
with fifty-six-inch drivers and cylinders big enough
to sit up and eat breakfast in.   Spick and span
both of them, just long enough out of the shops to
run smoothly to the work; and on Friday Oliver
Sollers, who, when he opened a throttle, blew miles
over the tender like feathers, took the 1012, groomed
like a Wilkes mare, down to Piedmont for the run
up to the Bend.

Now Oliver Sollers was a runner in a thousand,

and steady as a clock; but he had a fireman who could n't stand prosperity, Steve Horigan, a cousin of Johnnie's. The glory was too great for Steve, and he spent Friday night in Gallagher's place celebrating, telling the boys what the 1012 would do to the Yellow Mail. Not a thing, Steve claimed after five drinks, but pull the stamps clean off the letters the minute they struck the foot-hills. But when Steve showed up at five A.M. to superintend the movement, he was seasick. The minute Sollers set eyes on him he objected to taking him out. Mr. Sollers was not looking for any unnecessary chances on one of Bucks's personal matters, and for the general manager the Yellow Mail test had become exceedingly personal. Practically everybody East and West had said it would fail; Bucks said no.

Neighbor himself was on the Piedmont platform that morning, watching things. The McCloud despatchers had promised the train to our division on time, and her smoke was due with the rise of the sun. The big superintendent of Motive Power, watching anxiously for her arrival, and planning anx-

iously for her outgoing, glared at the bunged fireman
in front of him, and, when Sollers protested, Neighbor turned on the swollen Steve with sorely bitter
words. Steve swore mightily he was fit and could
do the trick — but what 's the word of a railroad
man that drinks? Neighbor spoke wicked words,
and while they poured on the guilty Steve's crop
there was a shout down the platform. In the east
the sun was breaking over the sandhills, and below
it a haze of black thickened the horizon. It was
McTerza with the 808 and the Yellow Mail.
Neighbor looked at his watch; she was, if anything,
a minute to the good, and before the car tinks could
hustle across the yard, a streak of gold cut the sea
of purple alfalfa in the lower valley, and the nar-
rows began to smoke with the dust of the race for
the platform.

When McTerza blocked the big drivers at the
west end of the depot, every eye was on the new
equipment. Three standard railway mail cars, done
in varnished buttercup, strung out behind the sizzling engine, and they looked pretty as cowslips.

While Neighbor vaguely meditated on their beauty and on his boozing fireman, Jimmie Bradshaw, just in from a night run down from the Bend, walked across the yard. He had seen Steve Horigan making a " sneak " for the bath-house, and from the yard gossip Jimmie had guessed the rest.

" What are you looking for, Neighbor ? " asked Jimmie Bradshaw.

" A man to fire for Sollers — up. Do you want it ? "

Neighbor threw it at him cross and carelessly, not having any idea Jimmie was looking for trouble. But Jimmie surprised him; Jimmie did want it.

" Sure, I want it. Put me on. Tired ? No. I 'm fresh as rainwater. Put me on, Neighbor; I 'll never get fast any other way. Doubleday would n't give me a fast run in a hundred years.

" Neighbor," cried Jimmie, greatly wrought, " put me on, and I 'll plant sunflowers on your grave."

There was n't much time to look around; the 1012 was being coupled on to the mail for the hardest run on the line.

"Get in there, you blamed idiot," roared Neighbor presently at Jimmie. "Get in and fire her; and if you don't give Sollers two hundred and ten pounds every inch of the way I'll set you back wiping."

Jimmie winked furiously at the proposition while it was being hurled at him, but he lost no time climbing in. The 1012 was drumming then at her gauge with better than two hundred pounds. Adam Shafer, conductor for the run, ran backward and forward a minute examining the air. At the final word from his brakeman he lifted two fingers at Sollers; Oliver opened a notch, and Jimmie Bradshaw stuck his head out of the gangway. Slowly, but with swiftly rising speed, the yellow string began to move out through the long lines of freight cars that blocked the spurs; and those who watched that morning from the Piedmont platform, thought a smoother equipment than Bucks's mail train never drew out of the mountain yards.

Jimmie Bradshaw jumped at the work in front of him. He had never lifted a pick in as swell a cab. The hind end of the 1012 was big as a private car; Jimmie had never seen so much play for a shovel in his life, and he knew the trick of his business better than most men even in West End cabs, the trick of holding the high pressure every minute, of feeling the drafts before they left the throttle ; and as Oliver let the engine out very, very fast, Jimmie Bradshaw sprinkled the grate bars craftily and blinked at the shivering pointer, as much as to say, " It 's you and me now for the Yellow Mail, and nobody else on earth."

There was a long reach of smooth track in front of the foothills. It was there the big start had to be made, and in two minutes the bark of the big machine had deepened to a chest tone full as thunder. It was all fun for an hour, for two hours. It was that long before the ambitious fireman realized what the new speed meant: the sickening slew, the lurch on lurch so fast the engine never righted, the shortened breath along the tangent, the giddy roll to the elevation and the sudden shock of the curve, the roar of the flight on

the ear, and, above and over it all, the booming
purr of the maddened steel. The canoe in the
heart of the rapid, the bridge of a liner at sea, the
gun in the heat of the fight, take something of
this — the cab of the mail takes it all.

When they struck the foothills Sollers and Jimmie Bradshaw looked at their watches and looked
at each other like men who had turned their backs
on every mountain record. There was a stop
for water, speed drinks so hard, an oil round, an
anxious touch on the journals; then the Yellow
Mail drew reeling into the hills. Oliver eased
her just a bit for the heavier curves, but for all
that the train writhed frantically as it cut the seg-
ments, and the men thought, in spite of themselves, of the mountain curves ahead. The worst
of the run lay ahead of the pilot, because the art
in mountain running is not alone or so much in
getting up hill; it is in getting down hill. But
by the way the Yellow Mail got that day up hill
and down, it seemed as if Steve Horigan's dream
would be realized, and that the 1012 actually

would pull the stamps off the letters. Before they knew it they were through the gateway, out into the desert country, up along the crested buttes, and then, sudden as eternity, the wheel-base of the 1012 struck a tight curve, a pent-down rail sprang out like a knitting-needle, and the Yellow Mail shot staggering off track into a gray borrow-pit.

There was a crunching of truck and frame, a crashing splinter of varnished cars, a scream from the wounded engine, a cloud of gray ash in the burning sun, and a ruin of human effort in the ditch. In the twinkle of an eye the mail train lay spilled on the alkali; for a minute it looked desperate bad for the general manager's test.

It was hardly more than a minute; then like ants out of a trampled hill men began crawling from the yellow wreck. There was more — there was groaning and worse, yet little for so frightful a shock. And first on his feet, with no more than scratches, and quickest back under the cab after his engineer, was Jimmie Bradshaw, the fireman.

Sollers, barely conscious, lay wedged between the tank and the footboard. Jimmie, all by himself, eased him away from the boiler. The conductor stood with a broken arm directing his brakeman how to chop a crew out of the head mail car, and the hind crews were getting out unaided. There was a quick calling back and forth, and the cry, "Nobody killed!" But the engineer and the conductor were put out of action. There was, in fact, only one West End man unhurt — Jimmie Bradshaw.

The first wreck of the fast mail, there have been worse since, took place just east of Crockett's siding. A west-bound freight lay at that moment on the passing track waiting for the mail. Jimmie Bradshaw, the minute he righted himself, cast up the possibilities of the situation. Before the freight crew had reached the wreck Jimmie was hustling ahead to tell them what he wanted. The freight conductor demurred; and when they discussed it with the freight engineer, Kingsley, he objected. "My engine won't never stand it; it'll pound her to scrap," he argued. " I reckon the safest thing to do is to get orders."

" Get orders!" stormed Jimmie Bradshaw, pointing at the wreck. " Get orders! Are you running an engine on this line and don't know the orders for those mail bags? The orders is to move 'em! That's orders enough. Move 'em! Uncouple three of those empty box-cars and hustle 'em back. By the Great United States! any man that interferes with moving this mail will get his time, that's what he'll get. That's Doubleday, and don't you forget it. The thing is to move the mail, not to stand here chewing about it!"

" Bucks wants the stuff hustled," put in the freight conductor, weakening before Jimmie's eloquence, " everybody knows that."

" Uncouple there!" cried Jimmie, climbing into the mogul cab. " I'll pull the bags, Kingsley; you need n't take any chances. Come back there, every mother's son of you, and help on the transfer."

He carried his points with a gale. He was con-

ductor and engineer and general manager all in
one.   He backed the boxes to the curve below
the spill, and set every man at work piling the mail
from the wrecked train to the freight cars.   The
wounded cared for the wounded, and the dead
might have buried the dead; Jimmie moved the
mail.   Only one thing turned his hair gray; the
transfer was so slow, it threatened to defeat his plan.
As he stood fermenting, a stray party of Sioux bucks
on a vagrant hunt rose out of the desert passes, and
halted to survey the confusion.   It was Jimmie
Bradshaw's opportunity.   He had the blanket men
in council in a trice.   They talked for one minute;
in two, he had them regularly sworn in and carrying second-class.   The registered stuff was jealously
guarded by those of the mail clerks who could still
hobble — and who, head for head, leg for leg, and
arm for arm, can stand the wrecking that a mail
clerk can stand ?   The mail crews took the registered matter; the freight crews and Jimmie, dripping
sweat and anxiety, handled the letter-bags; but second and third-class were temporarily hustled for the

Great White Father by his irreverent children of the Rockies.

Before the disabled men could credit their senses the business was done, they made as comfortable as possible, and, with the promise of speedy aid back to the injured, the Yellow Mail, somewhat disfigured, was heading again westward in the box-cars. This time Jimmie Bradshaw, like a dog with a bone, had the throttle. Jimmie Bradshaw for once in his life had the coveted fast run, and till he sighted Fort Rucker he never for a minute let up.

Meantime, at Medicine Bend, there was a desperate crowd around the despatcher. It was an hour and twenty minutes after Ponca Station reported the Yellow Mail out, before Fort Rucker, eighteen miles west, reported the box-cars and Jimmie Bradshaw in, and followed with a wreck report from the Crockett siding. When that end of it began to tumble into the Wickiup office Doubleday's face turned hard; fate was against him, the contract gone glimmering, and he did n't

feel at all sure his own head and the roadmaster's
would n't follow it. Then the Rucker operator
began again to talk about Jimmie Bradshaw, and
" Who 's Bradshaw ? " asked somebody ; and Rucker went on excitedly with the story of the mogul
and of three box-cars, and of a war party of Sioux
squatting on the brake-wheels ; it came so mixed
that Medicine Bend thought everybody at Rucker
Station had gone mad.

While they fumed, Jimmie Bradshaw was speeding the mail through the mountains. He had
Kingsley's fireman, big as an ox and full of his
own enthusiasm. In no time they were flying
across the flats of the Spider Water, threading the
curves of the Peace River, and hitting the rails of
the Painted Desert, with the mogul sprinting like
a Texas steer, and the box-cars leaping like year-
lings at the joints. It was no case of scientific running, no case of favoring the roadbed, of easing the
strain on the equipment ; it was simply a case of
galloping to a Broadway fire with a Silsby rotary
on a 4–11 call. Up hill and down, curve and

tangent, it was all one. There was speed made on the plains with that mail, and there was speed made in the foothills with the fancy equipment, but never the speed that Jimmie Bradshaw made when he ran the mail through the gorges in three box-cars; and frightened operators and paralyzed station agents all the way up the line watched the fearful and wonderful train, with Bradshaw's red head sticking out of the cab window, shiver the switches.

Medicine Bend could n't get the straight of it over the wires. There was an electric storm in the mountains, and the wires went bad in the midst of the confusion. They knew there was a wreck, and understood there was mail in the ditch, and, with Doubleday frantic, the despatchers were trying to get the track to run a train down to Crockett's. But Jimmie Bradshaw had asked at Rucker for rights to the Bend, and in an unguarded moment they had been given; after that it was all off. Nobody could get action on Jimmie Bradshaw. He took the rights, and stayed not for stake nor stopped not for

stone.   In thirty minutes the operating department
were wild to kill him, but he was making such time
it was concluded better to humor the lunatic than to
hold him up anywhere for a parley.   When this
was decided Jimmie and his war party were already
reported past Bad Axe, fifteen miles below the Bend
with every truck on the box-cars smoking.

The Bad Axe run to the Bend was never done in
less than fourteen minutes until Bradshaw that day
brought up the mail.   Between those two points the
line is modeled on the curves of a ram's horn, but
Jimmie with the mogul found every twist on the
right of way in eleven minutes; that particular
record is good yet.   Indeed, before Doubleday, then
in a frenzied condition, got his cohorts fairly on the
platform to look for Jimmie, the hollow scream of
the big freight engine echoed through the mountains.
Shouts from below brought the operators to the upper
windows; down the Bend they saw a monster locomotive flying from a trailing horn of smoke.   As the
stubby string of freight cars slewed quartering into
the lower yard, the startled officials saw them from

the Wickiup windows wrapped in a stream of flame. Every journal was afire, and the blaze from the boxes, rolling into the steam from the stack, curled hotly around a bevy of Sioux Indians, who clung sternly to the footboards and brake-wheels on top of the box-cars. It was a ride for the red men that is told around the council fires yet. But they do not always add in their traditions that they were hanging on, not only for life, but likewise for a butt of plug tobacco promised for their timely aid at Crockett siding.

By the time Jimmie slowed up his astounding equipment the fire brigade was on the run from the roundhouse. The Sioux warriors climbed hastily down the fire escapes, a force of bruised and bare-headed mail clerks shoved back the box-car doors, the car tinks tackled the conflagration, and Jimmie Bradshaw, dropping from the cab with the swing of a man who has done a trick, waited at the gangway for the questions to come at him. For a minute they came hot.

"What the blazes do you mean by bringing in

an engine in that condition ? " choked Doubleday, pointing to the blown machine.

"I thought you wanted the mail?" winked Jimmie.

"How the devil are we to get the mail with you blocking the track two hours?" demanded Callahan, insanely.

"Why, the mail's here, in these box-cars," answered Jimmie Bradshaw, pointing to his bobtail train. "Now don't look daffy like that; every sack is right here. I thought the best way to get the mail here was to bring it. Hm? We're forty minutes late, ain't we?"

Doubleday waited to hear no more. Orders flew like curlews from the superintendent and the master mechanic. They saw there was a life for it yet. Before the fire brigade had done with the trucks a string of new mail cars was backed down beside the train. The relieving mail crews waiting at the Bend took hold like cats at a pudding, and a dozen extra men helped them sling the pouches. The 1014, blowing porpoisewise, was backed up just as Benedict Morgan's train pulled down for Crockett's siding, and the Yellow Mail, rehabilitated, rejuvenated, and exultant, started up the gorge for Bear Dance, only fifty-three minutes late with Hawksworth in the cab.

" And if you can't make that up, Frank, you 're no good on earth," sputtered Doubleday at the engineer he had put in for that especial endeavor. And Frank Hawksworth did make it up, and the Yellow Mail went on and off the West End on the test, and into the Sierras for the coast, ON TIME.

" There 's a butt of plug tobacco and transportation to Crockett's coming to these bucks, Mr. Doubleday," wheezed Jimmie Bradshaw uncertainly, for with the wearing off of the strain came the idea to Jimmie that he might have to pay for it himself. " I promised them that," he added, " for helping with the transfer. If it had n't been for the blankets we would n't have got off for another hour. They chew Tomahawk, rough and ready preferred, Mr. Doubleday. Hm ? "

Doubleday was looking off into the yard.

" You 've been on a freight run some time, Jimmie," said he tentatively.

The Indian detachment was crowding in pretty
close on the red-headed engineer. He blushed.
" If you 'll take care of my tobacco contract,
Doubleday, we 'll call the other matter square.
I 'm not looking for a fast run as much as I
was."

" If we get the mail contract," resumed Doubleday reflectively, " and it won't be your fault if we
don't — hm ? — we may need you on one of the
runs. Looks to me as if you ought to have one."

Jimmie shook his head. " I don't want one,
don't mind me; just fix these gentlemen out with
some tobacco before they scalp me, will you ? "

The Indians got their leaf, and Bucks got his
contract, and Jimmie Bradshaw got the pick of the
runs on the Yellow Mail, and ever since he 's been
kicking to get back on a freight. But they don't
call him Bradshaw any more. No man in the
mountains can pace him on a run. And when the
head brave of the hunting party received the butt

of tobacco on behalf of his company, he looked at Doubleday with dignity, pointed to the sandy engineer, and spoke freckled words in the Sioux.

That's the way it came about. Bradshaw holds the belt for the run from Bad Axe to Medicine Bend; but he never goes any more by the name of Bradshaw. West of McCloud, everywhere up and down the mountains, they give him the name the Sioux gave him that day — Jimmie the Wind.

THE END